Apress Pocket Guides

Apress Pocket Guides present concise summaries of cutting-edge developments and working practices throughout the tech industry. Shorter in length, books in this series aims to deliver quick-to-read guides that are easy to absorb, perfect for the time-poor professional.

This series covers the full spectrum of topics relevant to the modern industry, from security, AI, machine learning, cloud computing, web development, product design, to programming techniques and business topics too.

Typical topics might include:

- A concise guide to a particular topic, method, function or framework

- Professional best practices and industry trends

- A snapshot of a hot or emerging topic

- Industry case studies

- Concise presentations of core concepts suited for students and those interested in entering the tech industry

- Short reference guides outlining 'need-to-know' concepts and practices.

More information about this series at `https://link.springer.com/bookseries/17385`.

Building Robust IT Release Processes

A Quick Guide for Designing a Scalable Software Delivery Framework

Yuri Kuznetsoff

Apress®

Building Robust IT Release Processes: A Quick Guide for Designing a Scalable Software Delivery Framework

Yuri Kuznetsoff
Burnaby, BC, Canada

ISBN-13 (pbk): 979-8-8688-2651-1 ISBN-13 (electronic): 979-8-8688-2652-8
https://doi.org/10.1007/979-8-8688-2652-8

Managing Director, Apress Media LLC: Welmoed Spahr
Acquisitions Editor: James Robinson-Prior
Editorial Assistant: Gryffin Winkler

Cover designed by eStudioCalamar

Distributed to the book trade worldwide by Springer Science+Business Media New York, 1 New York Plaza, New York, NY 10004. Phone 1-800-SPRINGER, fax (201) 348-4505, e-mail orders-ny@springer-sbm.com, or visit www.springeronline.com. Apress Media, LLC is a Delaware LLC and the sole member (owner) is Springer Science + Business Media Finance Inc (SSBM Finance Inc). SSBM Finance Inc is a **Delaware** corporation.

For information on translations, please e-mail booktranslations@springernature.com; for reprint, paperback, or audio rights, please e-mail bookpermissions@springernature.com.

Apress titles may be purchased in bulk for academic, corporate, or promotional use. eBook versions and licenses are also available for most titles. For more information, reference our Print and eBook Bulk Sales web page at http://www.apress.com/bulk-sales.

Any source code or other supplementary material referenced by the author in this book is available to readers on GitHub. For more detailed information, please visit https://www.apress.com/gp/services/source-code.

If disposing of this product, please recycle the paper

Table of Contents

About the Author

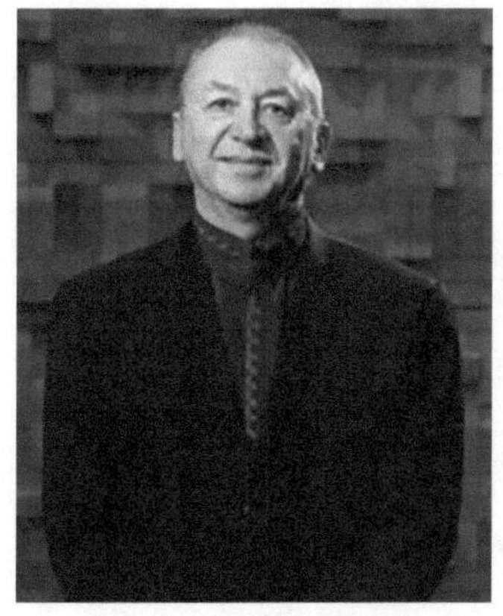

Yuri Kuznetsoff is a seasoned IT professional with over two decades of experience spanning software design, solution development, build automation, and enterprise release management. His career journey—from hands-on coding to orchestrating complex release pipelines—has given him a unique perspective on the challenges of modern software delivery. Yuri specializes in creating scalable, reliable, and repeatable release processes that bridge traditional methodologies with agile frameworks. He currently resides in Canada and is passionate about helping organizations mature their IT operations through practical, real-world strategies.

About the Technical Reviewer

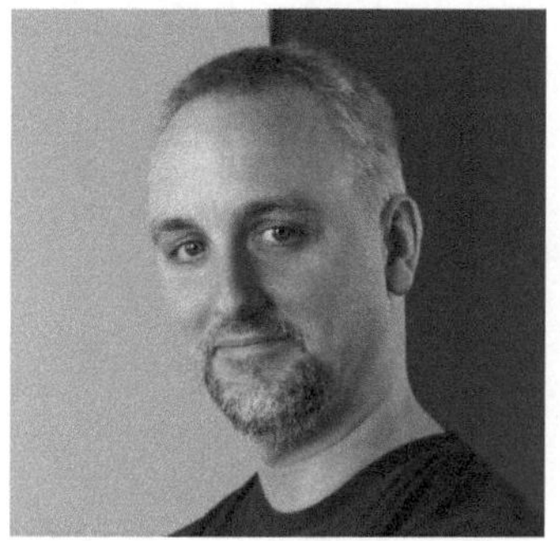 **Mauro Chojrin** is a technical coach and software development consultant, specialized in PHP. He has been involved in the IT industry since 1997 in a wide array of positions, including technical support, development, team leadership, IT management, and teaching. He also maintains his blog and YouTube channel, where he shares his knowledge with the world.

Introduction

Building Robust IT Release Processes is a practical, field-tested guide for designing, implementing, and operating reliable release, deployment, and disaster recovery processes across modern enterprise environments. Written for release managers, change managers, DevOps leads, SREs, and technical program managers, the book provides a comprehensive, real-world framework that strengthens delivery quality while maintaining governance, security, and operational stability.

The book covers the full spectrum of release methodologies—from traditional, scope-driven release cycles to Continuous Delivery and hybrid models that support both legacy systems and modern cloud-native applications. Readers learn how to define release structures, create Release Plans, implement consistent versioning, coordinate multi-team deliveries, run staging exercises, and execute production deployments with proper authorization, verification, and rollback readiness. A dedicated section outlines a complete infrastructure release process, including platform upgrades, security and compliance updates, infrastructure expansion, monitoring improvements, and Infrastructure-as-Code (IaC) workflows. It provides templates, checklists, environment validation practices, and risk management techniques essential for maintaining platform reliability.

The book also includes an extensive Disaster Recovery (DR) framework that integrates directly into release and infrastructure management workflows. Topics include DR governance, Recovery Time Objective (RTO) and Recovery Point Objective (RPO) planning, failover and failback execution, communication protocols, runbook requirements, service tiering, and regulatory alignment. A DR maturity model helps organizations assess and improve readiness. Dozen diagrams, decision trees, and step-by-step procedures illustrate complex processes in a clear, concise manner. Real-world case studies—from FinTech (Financial Technology), SaaS, and global enterprise environments—demonstrate how standardized release practices reduce risk, improve audit posture, and increase delivery speed.

This book provides everything an organization needs to build a scalable, auditable, and resilient release process that consistently delivers high-quality software and infrastructure changes.

Glossary

A

- **Artifact** – A compiled or packaged output of a build.

- **Availability Zone** – Independent data center within a cloud region.

B

- **Blue-Green Deployment** – Release strategy with two production environments.

- **Build (Code)** – A build is an artifact of building your source code from any branch through a build system (e.g., MAVEN, Jenkins). A successful build must have passed its tests and be installable or deployable to its environments.

- **Build Pipeline** – Automated compilation and testing sequence.

C

- **CAB (Change Advisory Board)** – Governance body for change approvals.

- **Canary Deployment** – Progressive rollout to a small user subset.

- **Change Management** – Controlled handling of system changes. Ensure standardized methods, processes, and procedures are used for all changes, to facilitate efficient and prompt handling of change and to maintain the proper balance between the need for change and the potential (risk) detrimental impact of change.

- **Change Request** – Formal request for system modification.

- **Cluster** – Group of servers managed as one.

- **CMDB** – Repository of configuration items.

- **Configuration Management** – Configuration management (CM) is a continuous process of recording and maintaining consistent and reliable records pertaining to an organization's hardware and software composition, including software version control and hardware update.

- **Configuration Management Database (CMDB)** – A CMDB is a centralized repository used in IT Service Management (ITSM) to store information about an organization's IT assets (hardware, software, and network elements), which are called configuration items (CIs). It also details the relationships and dependencies between these items, providing a comprehensive view of the entire IT infrastructure.

- **Continuous Delivery** – Automated delivery to staging.

- **Continuous Deployment** – Automated deployment to production.

- **Continuous Integration** – Automated code integration.

- **CI/CD** – Combined integration and delivery process. Continuous Integration is the automated (Jenkins and others) pipeline for software integration, verification, and promotion to release candidate (RC) build. Continuous Delivery is the delivery of the service to staging and production as part of the release process and is not considered the step immediately following Continuous Integration.

D

- **Declarative Configuration** – Define desired state.

- **Deployment** – Making software available in an environment.

- **Documentation** – Technical and user-facing material.

- **DORA Metrics** – DF, LT, CFR, MTTR.

- **Drift** — Infrastructure deviating from IaC.

E

- **Emergency Change** – Fast change to fix a major incident.

- **Environment** – A technological environment involving systems. References to "environment" will be specified as "production environment" or "test environment" where that distinction is relevant.

F

- **Failover** – Switching to redundant systems.

- **Feature Flag** – Toggle features at runtime.

- **Function** – Organizational department.

G

- **GitOps** – Managing infra via Git as source of truth.

H

- **High Availability** – Ensuring operation despite failures.

I

- **IAM** – Identity and Access Management.

- **IaC** – Infrastructure-as-Code.

- **Imperative Configuration** – Step-by-step IaC.

- **Incident** – Unplanned service disruption or the threat of the occurrence of such a disruption.

- **Interface** – A software interface is a shared boundary across which two or more separate software components exchange data, configuration, or state. Interface specification is a key piece of system architecture and software design.

- **Infrastructure Provisioning** – Automated infrastructure creation.

- **Infrastructure State File** – Tracks deployed resources.

L

- **Least Privilege** – Minimum required permissions.

O

- **Object Storage** – Distributed storage.

- **Observability** – Logs, metrics, traces for understanding systems.

P

- **Penetration Testing** – Simulated attack.

- **Process Owner** – The practical owner of a process who can authorize changes to the process and provide resource to support the implementation of changes to the process.

- **Provisioning** – Automated setup of resources.

- **Production Release** – A uniquely labeled bundle of features/functionalities, defined by the business, that may be made available for customer(s).

- **RPO** – Recovery Point Objective. The maximum acceptable data loss, measured in time.

Q

- **Quality Gate** – Required validation for promotion.

R

- **RBAC** – Role-Based Access Control.

- **RCA** – Root cause analysis.

- **Region** – Geographic cloud area.

- **Release Candidate** – A release candidate (RC) is a build with potential to be a final product, which is ready to release unless significant bugs emerge.

- **Release Vitals** – Document outlining release details.

- **Requirement** – Documented need or expectation, generally implied or obligatory.

- **Risk** – An estimation of the likelihood that a threat will create an undesirable impact. In terms of this method, risk may be expressed as the product of a likelihood and an impact.

- **RTO** – Recovery Time Objective. The maximum acceptable time it takes to restore a system or service after a disruption.

S

- **Scalability** – Capability to increase performance.

- **Security** – An assurance that characteristics of information assets are protected. Confidentiality, integrity, and availability are common security characteristics. Other characteristics of information assets such as velocity, authenticity, and reliability may also be considered if these are valuable to the organization and its constituents.

- **Serverless** – Execution without managing servers.

- **Service** – API-accessible reusable component. It is a provider of functionality with a purpose that different consumers can reuse for similar purposes, together with the policies that should control its usage (i.e., access rights, performance guarantees).

- **Showcase Environment** – Demo/training environment.

- **SLA/SLO/SLI** – Service agreements and metrics.

- **SRE** – Site Reliability Engineering.

- **Standard** – Something considered by an authority or by general consent as a basis of comparison; an approved model.

- **Standard Change** – Low-risk pre-approved change.

- **State File** – Infra tracking file.

V

- **Versioning (Business)** – Business-defined label.

- **Versioning (Technical)** – It is the process of assigning a unique label/identity to a unique state of software or component, e.g., a build, a release, a library, API, documentation, configurations, or other artifacts. The purpose of software versioning is to both archive and reproduce that unique state at any time. The version label should be ordered.

- **VPC** – Virtual Private Cloud.

- **Vulnerability** – System security weakness.

W

- **WAF** – Web Application Firewall.

Z

- **Zero Trust** – No implicit trust model.

CHAPTER 1

Traditional Release Process

Release Process Overview

The release process is a core component of IT Release Management, essential for organizations of all sizes and development methodologies. It defines a structured, scalable, and repeatable approach to distributing software and infrastructure changes across environments—including production. At its core, it's a coordinated sequence of cross-functional activities and documentation that ensures consistent, successful service delivery.

To avoid reinventing the wheel, align your release process with the Service Transition phase of the ITIL lifecycle (Figure 1-1), which encompasses change management, release and deployment, testing and validation, versioning, and knowledge management. (ITIL is a registered trademark of the Office of Government Commerce.)

While industry best practices offer valuable guidance, your release process should be tailored to your organization's specific structure, product, and operations. Blindly applying generic models without analyzing your unique business context can lead to unnecessary overhead and increased operational costs.

© Yuri Kuznetsoff 2026

Y. Kuznetsoff, *Building Robust IT Release Processes*, Apress Pocket Guides, https://doi.org/10.1007/979-8-8688-2652-8_1

Ultimately, your goal isn't to showcase methodological sophistication—it's to meet customer expectations efficiently, on time, and within budget.

Figure 1-1 provides an overview of the ITIL service management framework, illustrating how the core lifecycle stages–Service Strategy, Service Design, Service Transition, and Service Operation–interact within a continuous improvement cycle. Surrounding each stage are the key processes that support it, highlighting how ITIL integrates strategy, design, transition, and operational practices to deliver reliable and well-governed IT services.

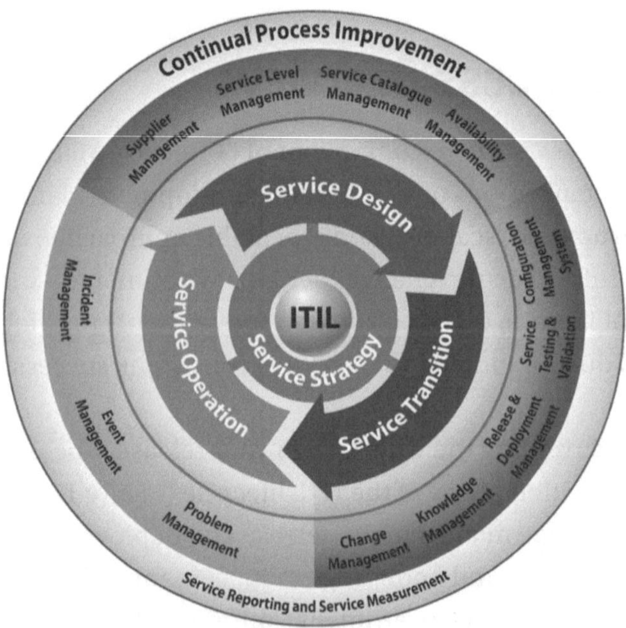

Figure 1-1. *The ITIL Service Lifecycle*

Release Process Objectives

The main objectives of the IT release process are as follows:

- Streamline service and infrastructure change distribution.

  - Offer an efficient release service that provides coordination between multiple stakeholders, change requestors, and solution developers.

  - Replace ad hoc decisions with standard processes where decisions are made automatically based on predefined criteria.

  - Reduce need for expensive and time-consuming meetings by moving action items to explicit plans where owners and approvers are assigned and each item status is tracked and visible to stakeholders.

- Increase change distribution process scalability, reliability, and reusability.

  - Distribute different release types to multiple environments in a timely manner.

  - Ensure that in case of a severe issue during the deployment, it is possible to roll back service(s) to previous stable version(s).

  - Keep the distribution process reusable by ensuring that all release actions and artifacts are well-defined and documented before they become part of the process.

- Ensure that only a fully authorized change is distributed to production.

  - Obtain IT Security Management approval for production releases.

  - Get Quality Assurance (QA) confirmation for all production releases.

  - Ensure that changed service performance is assessed by a subject matter expert and approved by the product owner.

  - Obtain Development, Quality Assurance (QA), Product, Project, and Support management approval for production releases.

- Ensure that the distribution process is transparent internally and auditable externally.

  - Categorize and document every change distributed to production.

  - Clearly separate generic and explicit release documentation. Generic documents detail policies, standards, processes, and procedures, while explicit plans are dynamic procedural documents that include action items and distribution instructions for specific release versions.

  - Create, manage, and execute release and deployment plans/tickets to completion for any change or set of changes that need to be released to production.

Release Process Types

Release process types classify the nature of the release (software, infrastructure, client app, microservice, etc.)

To release a change efficiently and reliably, define the following release process types:

- **Service/Software Release Process**

  Distributes

  - Code changes

  - Configuration changes

  - Database (DB) schema changes

- **Infrastructure Release Process**

  Coordinates

  - Operating system upgrades

  - Security patches/monitoring tools deployment

  - Infrastructure implementation for both new and existing services

  - Environment(s) setup

- **Client Application Release Process**

  - In addition to software and infrastructure release processes, you might want to define a simplified distribution process specific to a client mobile platform like iOS, Android, etc., whose deployment does not affect server side.

- **Sub-component/Microservice Release Process**

    - A sub-component/microservice release process
      is a simplified release process that regulates
      implementation and distribution of sub-
      component and/or microservice change, which
      does not affect customer experience so that user
      guide, impact notification, and other customer-
      facing actions/documentation are not required.

Define the Software Release Process

Start by defining the software release process type first, as it will become
the framework for all other processes you plan to develop.

Determine the Release Process Model

Release process models define the methodology and cadence used to
deliver the releases.

Senior Management should determine what kind of release model
your organization will use. This depends on your product specifics, IT and
engineering department's size, contractual/legal obligations, and budget.
Choose from the following release models:

a) Traditional Release Process that uses a scope-driven
    model, i.e., the release scope (list of features, fixes,
    and enhancements) is fairly static, but project
    schedule and resources are variable.

b) Continuous Delivery that uses a sprint-driven (period of time) model where schedule is constant, but scope and resources are variable. Continuous Delivery must be consistent, i.e., the development team should produce a fully verified production-ready release candidate (RC) at the end of every sprint, regardless of its frequency.

c) A combination of Traditional Release Process and Continuous Delivery. For example, Product and Marketing management are committed to deliver complex functionality to customers over a certain period of time, but the development team uses Continuous Delivery methodology in order to build and distribute an entire feature piece by piece. In this case I would recommend to create a two-layer process:

    i. Feature Release Process that coordinates customer-facing activities and documentation like marketing presentations, external notifications, customer training, feature flag that controls limited availability versus general availability, etc.

    ii. Service Delivery Process that coordinates continuous software delivery and deployment to the specific environments/containers using an automated pipeline like OpenShift Container Platform (OCP), a custom pipeline using Jenkins, etc.

In this model a required solution will be produced and distributed by multiple subsequent service deliveries.

When choosing a release process model, always prioritize common sense, practicality, and rationality.

- **Good Practices**

  - Using a traditional model for a highly regulated product where documentation, approvals, and customer-facing coordination require longer lead times

  - Selecting Continuous Delivery for a product with frequent incremental updates and a mature automated pipeline

  - Adopting a hybrid model when the business needs predictable customer-facing releases but engineering works in short sprints

- **Poor Practices**

  - Forcing Continuous Delivery on a team without automated testing or deployment tooling, resulting in unstable releases

  - Using a traditional model for a fast-moving SaaS product where long release cycles slow down customer value

- Choosing a model based on trendiness ("everyone is doing CD") rather than product constraints, team capacity, or compliance requirements

Define Release Process Structure

Next, you must define release process structure. It depends on the number of service/product types your company produces and number of development teams involved in building these services/products.

If your organization has a single development team, which produces one release candidate at a time, then you need to construct a single-layer release process.

If each service release is produced by multiple development teams that follow their own specifications and schedule, then you need to create a multi-layer release process that coordinates, orchestrates, and integrates multiple deliveries from different teams at different times.

Define Release Process Functions, Steps, and Artifacts

Figure 1-2 provides an end-to-end view of the software release lifecycle, showing how each functional group contributes to the process and which documents or tickets are produced at every stage. It maps activities from initial request through development, testing, staging, risk assessment, and production deployment, ensuring full visibility into responsibilities, required artifacts, and decision points across the release workflow.

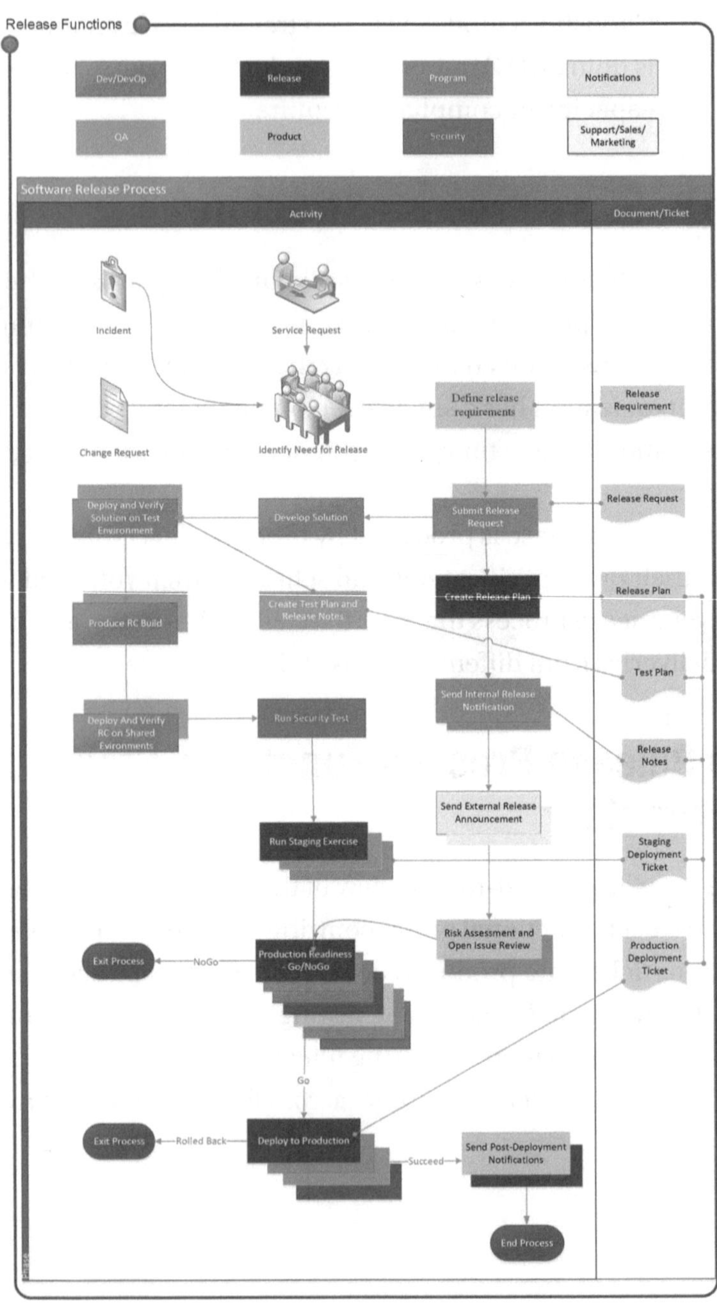

Figure 1-2. *Traditional Release Process Model*

Identify the Need for a Release

The need for a release should be identified by either Product Management or Change Management or Change Advisory Board (CAB) depending on your organizational structure.

A release is typically triggered by the need to

- Deliver new functionality to customers.

- Modify or fix existing functionality.

- Perform system maintenance, which may include software and/or infrastructure changes.

Release Requirements

Once a release need is identified, product owners must define its general characteristics. This impacts the scope of work and determines which teams and stakeholders must be involved.

- Product and Program management should define the release scope, including a list of features and fixes, and the target release date.

- In organizations with multiple integrated product lines, each product line owner should present their release scope to Senior Management or Enterprise Product Management for review.

Once the release features, target date, and affected development teams are confirmed, a Release Vitals document must be created. It should include

- Business drivers

- Development team(s)

- Key features/functionalities

- Links to related documents

- Target dates

Technical product and/or program managers are responsible for creating the Release Vitals content for their respective services. For releases involving multiple teams, each affected team lead must provide all necessary documentation about their service changes to the program manager.

Product owners must ensure that the Release Vitals document remains current throughout the development and distribution phases.

Determine Release Type

While many technical activities are consistent across release types, documentation, communication, training, and marketing requirements vary significantly. Releases are categorized by complexity as follows:

- **Major Release** – Introduces a new service or significantly enhances an existing one, often involving architectural changes

- **Enhancement** – Adds new features with limited impact, typically affecting specific user groups

- **Maintenance** – Resolves minor issues or implements customer-specific features not available to other users

- **Patch** – Addresses specific issues that must be resolved before the next maintenance release

- **Hotfix** – Implements critical security patches or urgent fixes to prevent or resolve service-impacting issues

For multi-component releases

- The release type does not depend on the number of components involved (e.g., a Major Release may involve one or many components).

- Regardless of release type, each development team must submit a release candidate (RC) for integration, performance, and security verification before production deployment.

Determine Release Version

An entity identifier plays a vital role in the IT world, so it requires common standards and consistent versioning policy to build efficient and scalable release and deployment processes.

Standardized versioning is critical, especially in financial organizations, where certain version increments often require compliance certification.

I would recommend using the following criteria when assigning a release version:

- Release version digits should be separated with dots (.), e.g., 1.0.0.0.

- The version number for any release type should always be fully qualified and reflect the release type: <major>.<minor/enhancement>.<service pack/ maintenance>.<patch/hotfix>, e.g., 1.2.3.4.

  It will ensure consistency and make it easy for automated release tracking and deployment tools to read and interpret it correctly.

- The version should include a service name or its acronym as an alphanumeric prefix, which is separated from the number by a hyphen (-), e.g., hello_world-1.2.2.33, my_service-1.2.1.48, etc.

- The major number for production releases should start from 1—not from 0. However, there might be cases where the development team wants to release a test service version that will not be consumed either by customers or by other production services. In this case, the version's first digit can be zero (0.1.1.1) to indicate the pre-production nature of the release.

- When the major number has incremented, all subsequent numbers should be reset to zero.

- When the minor/enhancement number has incremented, all subsequent numbers should be reset to zero as well.

- When the maintenance/service pack number has incremented, the patch/hotfix number should be preserved because it is an actual build number.

- When you release a patch or hotfix, a build number (fourth digit) reflects version increase.

Release Request

Each release request must be submitted to Release Management by the product owner or their delegate using a standard request form (e.g., wiki page or ticket). The request must include the following:

1) **Service Name and Version**

The service full name or its acronym followed by a unique version should be provided.

Please see the section "Determine Release Version" for details.

2) **Release Type**

Please see the section "Determine Release Type" for details.

3) **Release Description**

The summary of the release package content, i.e., which features or part of the features are being distributed to production—plus, if it includes any bug fixes.

4) **Release Scope**

List of all changes that are included in this release. It can be a URL to Internal Release Notes.

5) **Release Dependency**

If the release depends on any other releases or vice versa, all dependencies should be provided along with their release versions.

If the release depends on any infrastructure change that must be implemented either prior to or during or right after the production deployment, corresponding tasks should be provided.

6) **Release Candidate Target Date**

The release candidate (RC) target date must be provided. The RC target date cannot be later than the staging deployment date.

7) **Deployment Date/Time**

Estimated production and staging (if applicable) deployment date/time.

8) **Deployment Duration**

Estimated deployment duration.

9) **Release Target Date**

The release target date is the date when new functionality will be available to customers.

Feature flag or other functionality activation mechanism can be used to enable release either for a limited number of users (limited availability) or for all users (general availability).

New changes can be pre-deployed and tested on production environments before official release, with customer feature flag turned off.

10) **Potential Service Interruptions and Customer Impact**

Planned service outage or any potential of even a brief service interruption should be provided.

11) **Release Contacts**

As minimum team lead, DevOps, and QA contacts should be provided.

12) **Program (If Applicable)**

If the release is part of a bigger program or initiative, the name of that program/initiative should be provided.

Once Release Management receives the request, the assigned release manager will

- Set the request status to **In Progress**.

- Validate the release type and advise if adjustments are needed.

- Confirm sufficient time exists to process the release.

- Assess resource and environment availability and determine feasibility of the target date.

  If disagreements arise, escalate to Product Management.

If the release does not conflict with other deliveries

- Approve the request and notify stakeholders.

  Outcome – APPROVED—Approved as-is

If conflicts exist

- Discuss resolution with request owners.

  Possible Outcomes

- **COMBINED** – Released with another service on the requested date

- **MERGED** – Merged with an upcoming planned release of the same service

- **POSTPONED** – Delayed to a new target date

- **PARKED** – Delayed with no new target date

- Once the release request is Approved as-is, Release Management will create a Release Plan, add a corresponding record to the *Release Tracker* (see section "Create and Maintain a Release Tracker"), and set the release request status to **COMPLETE**.

- When the release has been deployed to production, the corresponding request record should be archived.

Release Plan

To plan, document, and track the progress of each release item, Release Management should create and maintain a Release Plan.

I would recommend using two different formats to document a variety of release types.

a) Release Plan format 1 should be used for major, minor/enhancement, and maintenance (release pack) release types. It is a comprehensive release checklist that includes the following sections:

  - *Summary* is a table that contains Major Release attributes.

  - *Major Milestones* is self-descriptive; it is a table that holds target dates for release milestones.

  - *Development Team Deliveries* is a matrix that contains the details for each development team release candidate.

- *Release Items* is a table where each record shows the details for the single Release Work Item. In terms of activity types, Release Work Items are categorized as follows:

  - Planning

  - Development/QA

  - Deployment

  - Documentation

  - Training

  - Notification

b) Release Plan format 2 is used for patch or hotfix release types. It is a simple release checklist that includes three sections:

- *Development Team Deliveries* is a matrix that contains release-related details for each development team with the corresponding ticket(s).

- *Release Items* is a table where each record includes the details for the single Release Work Item with the corresponding tickets (if applicable). If a patch or hotfix affects a single component, the activity should be performed by a component-level actor, i.e., project/product manager, QA lead, etc. Release owners might decide to run integration tests on shared environments and production post-deployment smoke tests. For urgent hotfix items, the approver can delegate item authorization to an appointed person.

- *Deployment* includes deployment steps and have reference to the ticket(s) that include deployment and verification instructions.

The release manager ensures that the Release Plan remains current throughout a release lifecycle. Any significant change or critical delay of completion of the working items should be communicated to stakeholders immediately.

Release Plan Example

This example is used for multi-servers integrated releases.

1) **Release Summary**

Note   The table is pre-populated with example values.

Version	SrvApp-1.0.1.1
Type	Maintenance
Scope	Multi-component
Status	PLANNED

2) **Release Status Definition**

   PLANNED

   IN PROGRESS

   COMPLETE

   CANCELED

3) **Action Item Status Definition**

PENDING – Work on release item/document did not start.

WIP – Work in progress.

DONE – Item/document has been completed and waits for approval.

ACCEPTED – Item/document has been accepted by approver.

WAIVED – Item/document is not relevant for this release.

4) **Key Release Milestones**

Note   The Status column is pre-populated with an initial value.

Milestone	Status	Due Date	Comments
All Component RCs Completed	PENDING		
All Component RCs Deployed to Shared Test Environment	PENDING		
Customer Notification Sent	PENDING		
Staging Initial Deployment Complete	PENDING		
Staging Rollback Complete	PENDING		
Integrated Testing Complete	PENDING		Include functionality, performance, and security testing.

(continued)

Milestone	Status	Due Date	Comments
Staging Final Deployment Complete	PENDING		
Production Deployment Complete	PENDING		
External Notification Sent	PENDING		

5)   Development Team/Component Release Items

Note   The checkmark followed by date in the *RC Actual Date* field signifies that RC has been completed and the Build Acceptance Checklist has been reviewed and accepted.

Service/Component Name	Release Type	Release Version	QA Test Plan	QA Test Plan Status

5a)   Development Team/Component Release Items (Continuation)

Build Acceptance Checklist	RC Target Date	RC Actual Date	Owners (Product/ Project)	Comments

6)   Release Process Functions, Steps, and Artifacts

Note   Release Work Items in the release checklist grouped by Activity Type are *not* in exact sequential order. Multiple activities can go in parallel.

Activity Type	Release Work Item	Owner	Approver	Status
Planning	Release Vitals Page	Product/ Program Manager	Product Owner	PENDING
Planning	Initial Risk Assessment	QA Lead	Product Owner	PENDING
Planning	Functional Test Plan	QA Lead	QA Manager	PENDING
Planning	Performance Test Plan	Performance Test Specialist	QA Manager	PENDING
Planning	Security Test Plan	Security Test Lead	Security Manager	PENDING
Planning	Release Plan	Release Manager	Enterprise Release Manager	PENDING
Planning	Deployment Plan	Release Manager	Enterprise Release Manager	PENDING
Development/QA	Deploy to Shared QA Environment	Environment Administrator	Environment Owner	PENDING
Development/QA	Integrated QA Testing Complete	QA Lead	QA Manager	PENDING

(continued)

Activity Type	Release Work Item	Owner	Approver	Status
Development/QA	Performance Testing Complete	Performance Test Specialist	QA Lead	PENDING
Development/QA	Security Testing Complete	Security Test Lead	Security Manager	PENDING
Release/ Deployment	Coordinate Deployment Schedule with Ops	Release Manager	Director of IT Operations	PENDING
Release/ Deployment	Staging Deployment Started	DevOps and QA Leads	Release Manager	PENDING
Release/ Deployment	Staging Deployment Complete	DevOps and QA Leads	Release Manager	PENDING
Release/ Deployment	Deploy to Production	Release Manager	Senior Product Management	PENDING
Release/ Deployment	Deploy to Showcase Environment (if applicable)	Environment Administrator	Environment Owner	PENDING
Documentation	Internal Release Notes	QA Lead	Support Manager	PENDING
Documentation	Update Release Tracker	Release Manager	Release Manager	PENDING
Documentation	Update Environments Wiki (if applicable)	Release Manager	Enterprise Release Manager	PENDING
Training	Internal Training	Appointed Instructor	Product Owner	PENDING

(continued)

Activity Type	Release Work Item	Owner	Approver	Status
Training	Customer Training	Appointed Instructor	Product Owner	PENDING
Notification	Send QA Release Notes Internally	QA Lead	QA Manager	PENDING
Notification	Send Documentation Internally	Tech Writer	Product Manager	PENDING
Notification	Send Documentation to Customers	Tech Writer	Product Owner	PENDING
Notification	Send Internal Release Announcement	Product Owner/ Tech Writer	Release Manager	PENDING
Notification	Send Customer Release Announcement	Product Owner/ Tech Writer	Release Manager	PENDING
Production Approval	Open Issue Review	Project Manager	Product Owner	PENDING
Production Approval	Potential Risk Assessment	Project Manager	Product Owner	PENDING
Production Approval	Release Final Approval (Go/NoGo)	Release Manager	All Stakeholders	PENDING
Production Retrospective	Retrospective Review Meeting	Release Manager	All Stakeholders	PENDING

6a)   **Release Process Functions, Steps, and Artifacts**

Note   The table in item **6a** is a direct continuation of the table in item **6**. For layout purposes, items **6** and **6a** together constitute a single table. The table in item **6a** should be merged to the right of the corresponding main table in item **6**, and they should read as one continuous table.

Target Date	Complete Date	Link/Ticket	Comments

Deployment Plan

Pre-deployment Steps

Send Out Internal Deployment Warning

- Send an email that contains an ETA for the overall deployment process.

Create a Chat Room

Create a deployment chat and invite deployment participants (DevOps, QA, dev lead, etc.)

stg1: <check box>

prod: <check box>

Deployment Steps

stg1: execute < Deployment Ticket>

prod: execute < Deployment Ticket>

Rollback Steps

stg1: execute Rollback section of < Deployment Ticket>

prod: execute Rollback section of < Deployment Ticket> **only if deployment failed**

Post-deployment Steps

Run Post-deploy Verification

stg1: <check box>

prod: <check box>

Archive Production Deployment Logs

- Save deployment communication logs for retrospective and auditing purposes. It can be attached to a corresponding deployment ticket.

Send Out Internal Deployment Confirmation

- Send email/text that confirms to stakeholders that deployment either has been successfully deployed or rolled back to the pre-deployment state.

Release Build

As part of a release lifecycle, development team(s) should produce and submit to Release Management a release build for further promotion and authorization.

Feature complete build, *release candidate,* and *final release candidate* are three main states that signify release build readiness for production deployment.

1) **Feature Complete Build**

A build is called *feature complete* (FC) when the development team agrees that no entirely new functionality will be added to this release. There could still be source code changes to fix defects, changes to documentation and data files, and peripheral code for test cases or utilities.

The development team should submit a build that meets FC acceptance criteria to Release Management. The build must be ready for

- Showcasing

- System-level verification:

  - Performance testing

  - Security testing

  - Functional end-to-end testing

2) **Release Candidate**

A *release candidate* (*RC*) is a build with potential to be a final product, which is ready to release unless significant bugs emerge. In this stage of product stabilization, all product features have been designed, coded, and tested with no known showstopper-class bug.

The development team *must* submit RC to the release manager for staging exercise and production deployment.

- RC should be deployable by DevOps, using deployment instructions.

Deployment instructions must be prepared and provided by the development team. These instructions enable DevOps to deploy the release candidate consistently across staging and production environments.

A typical deployment instruction package includes

- Deployment steps

- A clear, ordered sequence of actions required to deploy the build (e.g., scripts to execute, configuration updates, environment variables to set)

- Prerequisites

- Any infrastructure, services, feature flags, or external dependencies that must be in place before deployment begins

- Rollback procedure

- Steps to revert to the previous stable version, including any data restoration or configuration reversal required

- Verification steps

- Post-deployment checks to confirm the application is functioning correctly (smoke tests, endpoints to validate, log entries to review)

- Special considerations

- Known risks, temporary workarounds, or environment-specific notes that DevOps should be aware of during deployment

- The build is ready for

  - Staging initial deployment and verification

  - Staging rollback and verification

3) **Final Release Candidate**

A *final release candidate* (final RC) is a build where all issues are either fixed or deferred to the next release(s). The build is ready for

- Final staging roll-forward

- Production deployment

Submit Release Candidate

For each *major* or *enhancement* release type, the development team lead should create a RC Acceptance Checklist and submit it to Release Management.

The following items should be provided:

1. Explicit release type, i.e., major, minor, maintenance, patch or hotfix.

2. Standard fully qualified release build version.

3. Link to deploy and rollback instructions for staging and production deploys.

4. Link to Release Notes for this release.

5. Link to QA Test Plan.

6. List of tested component dependencies and their versions.

7. List of configuration additions and updates that are required to be done for your component in this release.

8. Link to test cases that were executed by the development team against this build. These test cases shall not be overwritten by future test case runs.

9. Who will run and verify the deployment to QA, staging, production, and Showcase environments.

10. Name of the development team lead who has signed off on this build.

The release manager should review the content of the submitted *RC Acceptance Checklist* and make sure that all acceptance criteria are met. Each time RC has been rebuilt

- QA lead ensures that the new, fully qualified RC version is stated in all QA-related tickets.

- Dev and QA leads should update the fully qualified RC version in the *RC Acceptance Checklist*.

- Development team should resubmit the new RC version to the release manager along with the updated *RC Acceptance Checklist*.

- Release manager should review the content of the resubmitted *RC Acceptance Checklist* and make sure that all acceptance criteria are met.

For maintenances, patches, and hotfixes, a simple ticket can be submitted instead where the change (code, configuration, db) and its QA coverage are documented.

Each time RC has been rebuilt

- QA lead should update corresponding tickets with the new RC version that passed the QA test and resubmit RC to the release manager.

- Assigned release manager should update the fully qualified RC version stated in all corresponding release and deployment artifacts.

Deploy RC on Pre-production and Showcase Environments

The number of pre-production and showcase environments that should be updated with the new RC version depends on company size, application complexity, and customer requirements. The release build might be just a simple client application, which is planned to be installed on user devices, or it might be a complex service that has to be deployed to thousands of nodes on multiple data centers across the globe.

It is vital to use automated deployment to upgrade multiple environments with a new service version. Otherwise, it would be an expensive and time-consuming manual exercise.

Here is the list of minimum pre-production and showcase environments recommended for release build installation and verification prior to production deployment:

- **Integrated QA** – Environment where the QA team runs cross-component end-to-end functional integration and regression testing.

- **Alpha/Beta Showcase** – Environment where the alpha or beta release version is deployed and used for internal training and external showcasing.

- **Staging** – Environment where infrastructure is as close to production as possible. It is used for final RC deployment, rollback, and post-deploy/rollback verification.

Senior Management might want to establish more environment types, i.e., user acceptance test (UAT), performance testing, etc.; however, I would strongly recommend, as minimum, to deploy and verify your RC on the listed above environments before deploying release to production.

I recommend assigning members of the Release Management team to administrate pre-prod environments.

The pre-prod environment administrator should coordinate service deployments and infrastructure implementations on corresponding environments to keep them up to date. Also, the administrator should create and maintain a documentation and/or dashboard where all essential information is captured.

Release Verification and Authorization

In order to make the Release Verification and Authorization process efficient, it should be well-defined and appropriately structured. RC should not be accepted until verification and authorization have been successfully completed and confirmation is stated in a corresponding ticket/artifact.

QA Functional Verification

For major and enhancement release types, the QA lead should create a Test Plan and present it to the relevant stakeholders for review and sign-off.

For maintenance, patch, or hotfix releases, QA test coverage can be documented in a corresponding ticket, which should be attached to a Release Plan. It is highly recommended for audit purposes to state a fully qualified component release version that passed the QA test. In this case Release Management has documented evidence that the release build planned for production deployment has passed QA verification.

The QA specialist executes tests on dedicated test environments following approved test cases.

Discovered issues should be triaged by the product owner or their delegate and either deferred to the next release or addressed in the next RC.

Performance Test

It is really important to make sure that application performance match acceptance criteria when new features are introduced or existing functionality enhanced.

Every development team should test the performance of each new service and make sure that the test is passed.

For multi-component releases, integrated cross-component performance testing should run on dedicated shared environments where production conditions/maximum load can be reproduced.

Security Test

It is paramount for any type of organization to ensure that the new version of software does not reduce system security level.

For each new release, the security specialist should review change scope and decide what test type is required, e.g., whether a security scan needs to run or just a new code review is sufficient. After reviewing all discovered deficiencies, the security specialist should report any issues to the corresponding product owner and determine which issue should be fixed immediately and which can be deferred to the next release.

In large organizations the senior security manager should review the security assessment report and authorize the release candidate for production deployment.

Open Issue Review

An Open Issue Review should be run for all releases.

All known issues that will be distributed to production as part of the release should be stated in a specific section of Internal Release Notes.

All open defects (including ones deferred to the next release) should be reviewed by the product owner and QA lead and approved before the Go/NoGo decision.

Internal Release Notes

Internal Release Notes is a primary release artifact and should be created for all production releases. This document lists all changes that are included in the release, including recent features, enhancements, bug fixes, and known issues. Stakeholders and affected personnel should review the changes prior to every production release and get their potential concerns addressed.

Internal Release Notes is only for internal reference, it is not documentation that is delivered to the customer, nor does it serve as a substitute for user guides.

The final version of *Internal Release Notes* should be sent to Support Management to ensure that help desk personnel are aware of the upcoming changes and prepared to take potential calls related to the upcoming release.

Customer Release Announcement

A Customer Release Announcement, which includes release date and time, type, change description, and customer impact, should be required for *all* release types.

It is recommended to make external notification available to customers a minimum of

- Five business days in advance of the **Major Release** production deployment.

- Two business days in advance of the **minor or maintenance release** production deployment.

- One business day in advance of the **patch release** production deployment.

- For **emergency hotfix,** customers *should* be retroactively notified within one business day (if there wasn't any opportunity to notify affected customers before hotfix deployment).

It is recommended to notify customers only about those releases that have material impact, e.g., service interruption, new functionality that requires a user guide, etc.

Internal Release Announcement

An Internal Release Announcement should be required for *all* release types.

The Internal Release Announcement should include the release type, release version, release date and time, change description, service interruption detail, and link to the finalized and approved *Internal Release Notes*.

The product owner or their delegate (QA lead) should send the Internal Release Announcement to all stakeholders no later than two business days in advance of the production deployment.

For hotfixes, an Internal Release Announcement can be sent within one business day after production deployment.

Staging Exercise

Each change *should* be deployed and verified on a staging environment before it hits production. The main goal of this exercise is to reproduce as close as possible production deployment, rollback, and post-deploy/rollback verification.

The staging exercise evaluates software deployability to multiple data centers (if applicable), multi-component deployment orchestration, and effectiveness of the communication channel.

Staging Deployment Procedure

Standard staging deployment procedure *should* include the following steps:

- QA runs a pre-deploy automated smoke test to ensure that legacy issues will not be mixed with potential deployment issues.

- DevOps deploys new code and/or configuration change to the staging environment using explicit deployment instructions.

- QA runs production-like post-deployment verification.

- DevOps rolls back deployed code and/or configuration change to the previous version using rollback instructions.

- QA runs production-like post-rollback verification.

- DevOps deploys new code and/or configuration change to the staging environment again using finalized deployment instructions.

Staging Deployment Ticket Structure

The staging deployment ticket should include assigned DevOps, QA, dev lead, and IT support specialist (if needed) names.

It should include explicit instructions or a link to the instruction page for all staging procedure steps, i.e., deployment instruction, post-deployment smoke test cases, rollback instruction, post-rollback verification instructions, etc.

Risk Management

Risk assessment should be done for all release types.

Each risk should be associated with a mitigation strategy. If mitigation is not possible, the open risk(s) should be accepted by the product owner before the release Go/NoGo decision.

Relevant product managers are responsible for follow-ups around risks and for keeping the risk management page up to date.

Production Release Approval

All items on the Release Plan should be completed prior to production deployment. Any showstopper issues should be satisfactorily addressed for the release to go forward.

The release manager should make the Go/NoGo decision when all active release items that should be done prior to production deployment are completed. If one of the showstopper items is still pending at the deployment time, Release Management should block the release and communicate the blocking issue to the product owner and relevant stakeholders.

Production Deployment

Production deployment is a vital function of the release process and explicitly defined in the Deployment Plan, which is a procedural delta document that details deployment prerequisites, orchestration, and pre-deployment, deployment, and post-deployment steps including owner(s) of each action.

For all releases the release manager adds a *Deployment Steps* section to the Release Plan.

For large and complex multi-component deployments, the release manager can create a separate *Deployment Plan* document as a child to the Release Plan.

The release manager initiates and tracks the completion of each step stated in the Deployment Plan.

Once all release items that should be done prior to production deployment are completed, the release manager provides the Go/NoGo confirmation. If there are no objections or concerns, the release manager states in the corresponding deployment ticket that it is a Go and sets ticket status to Ready for Deploy.

The release manager opens the deployment communication channel either using multi-party conversation in a desktop message app (recommended) or using corresponding deployment ticket comments and initiates the deployment procedure:

- Release manager confirms in the communication channel that it is a Go to deploy and verify the release build.

- QA runs pre-deploy automated smoke test(s) to ensure that legacy issues will not be mixed with potential deployment issues.

- Assigned DevOps deploys release build(s) to corresponding environments according to deployment instructions.

- QA runs post-deployment verification.

- Both DevOps and QA confirm that deployment either has been successfully completed or service must be rolled back to the pre-deployment state.

- If deployment has been successfully completed, the release manager states it in all corresponding artifacts.

- If service needs to be rolled back, DevOps rolls back the deployed build to the previous version using rollback instructions (please see section "Rollback Procedure" for details).

- QA runs post-rollback verification.

- Service owner notifies the stakeholders that deployment either was successfully completed or rolled back to the pre-deployment state.

Figure 1-3 illustrates the basic flow of the deployment procedure.

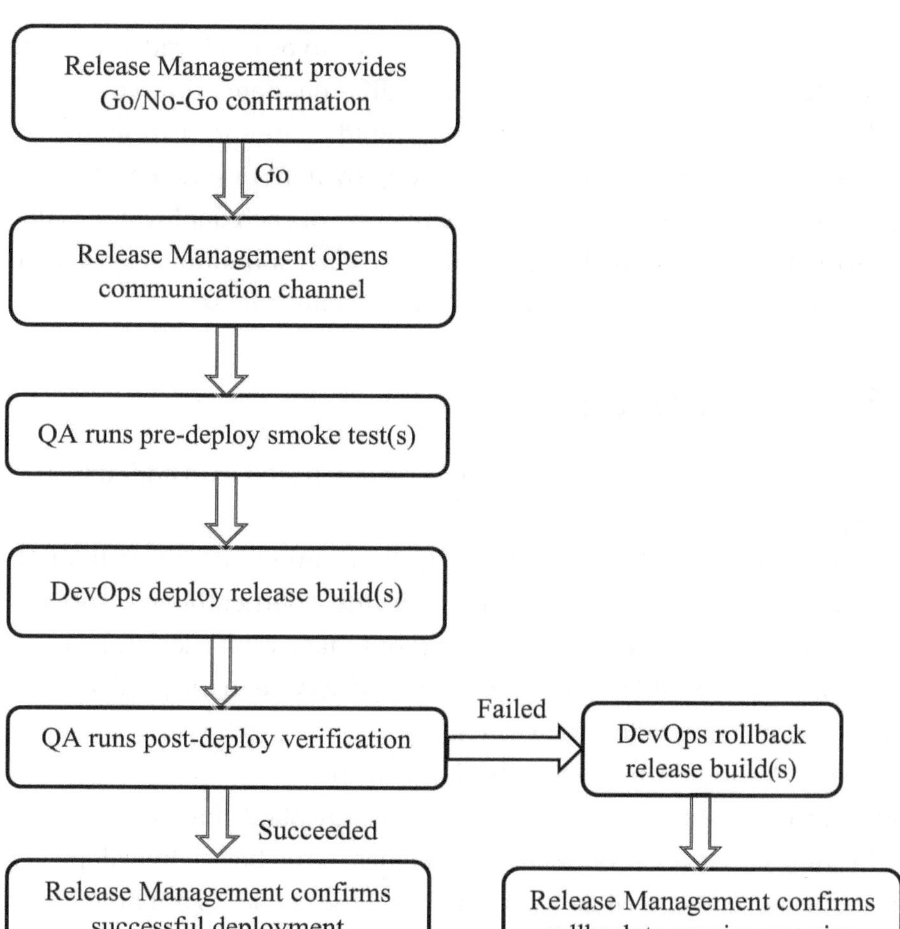

Figure 1-3. *Deployment Procedure Flowchart*

All deployment actions should be explicitly stated in the communication channel.

Deployment tickets and communication logs are not just essential operational and auditable artifacts but also provide vital information for all kinds of stats and analytics.

Multiphase Deployment

There might be cases where the same RC needs to be deployed to multiple data centers located in different regions at different dates/times or you need to deploy an existing production RC build on new infrastructure. In this case you should create a separate deployment ticket for each event in order to track progress and completion of each deployment. All deployment tickets should be attached to the corresponding Release Plan so it's easy to locate all artifacts related to a specific release.

Rollback Procedure

Explicit rollback instructions should be created, tested, and added to a corresponding deployment ticket.

If during deployment a blocking issue that cannot be troubleshooted is discovered, the product owner should decide whether the new service version needs to be rolled back. If it turns out that a rollback is the only option, DevOps should roll back the deployed service to the previous stable version using rollback instructions.

Then QA should run post-rollback verification to make sure that the rollback completed successfully and service is available for users.

In some cases, the product owner decides to roll back a fully deployed service because after a while it turns out that the service is not functioning on production as expected.

In this case, the following steps should happen:

- Product owner provides the reason for rollback in the corresponding deployment ticket.

- Release manager sets the deployment ticket status to Rollback and confirms that it is a Go to roll back the current production version to the previous one.

- DevOps rolls back the deployed service to the previous stable version using rollback instructions.

- QA runs post-rollback verification to make sure that rollback is completed successfully and service is available for users.

- Product owner sends the Internal Release Announcement to all stakeholders that were previously notified about the upcoming release, explaining why the current production version of the service was rolled back.

Release Retrospective

A regular Release Retrospective Meeting should be held after each major or minor release deployment to production. The product owner can call a Retrospective Meeting after any problematic release and run root cause analyses.

The stakeholders should review the release execution plan and identify possibilities for future improvement.

Create and Maintain a Release Tracker

I recommend to create and maintain a Release Tracker where you can track all upcoming releases, all releases that are in progress, and all completed releases.

A Release Tracker should be a table that includes Service Name, Release Version, Release Type, Link to Release Notes, Target Date, Release Date, Status, and Link to Release and Deployment Plan.

Release Statuses

- **PENDING** – Release activities are not started yet.

- **WIP** – Release is in progress.

- **COMPLETE** – Release has been successfully deployed and verified on production.

- **PARKED** – Release postponed with no new target date.

- **MERGED** – Release merged with an upcoming planned release of the same service.

- **ROLLEDBACK** – Service has been rolled back to the previous stable version.

Once the Release Tracker is created and maintained, Release Management can see all upcoming, current, and completed releases' status and corresponding essential details.

Case Study: Traditional Release in a Regulated Financial and Technology Organization

Background

A mid-sized FinTech (Financial Technology) company operating across North America was required to comply with strict regulatory standards such as SOC 2 (https://secureframe.com/hub/soc-2/what-is-soc-2), PCI-DSS (https://www.pcisecuritystandards.org/standards/pci-dss/), and regional financial regulations. Releases contained sensitive transaction-processing logic distributed across several microservices.

Problem Statement

A high-impact quarterly Major Release involved seven integrated services, database schema changes, and a new fraud detection module. Previous releases suffered delays due to missing artifacts, inconsistent QA coverage, and last-minute dependency conflicts.

Approach

To stabilize the release cycle, the organization implemented a unified Traditional Release Process with a standardized Release Plan, RC Acceptance Checklist, and mandatory regression coverage. All participating teams were required to provide consistent versioning, staging deployment instructions, and post-deploy verification steps.

Traditional Release Coordination Basic Flow

Figure 1-4 outlines the sequential workflow used in traditional release coordination.

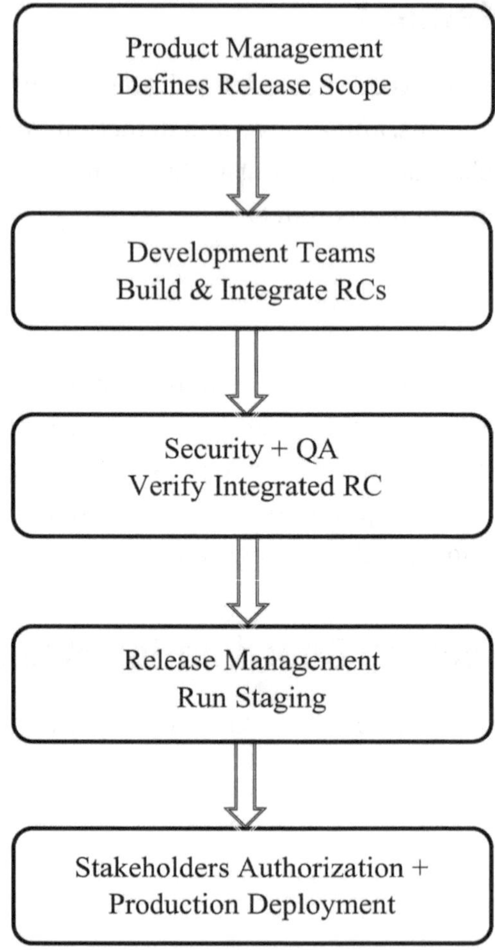

Figure 1-4. *Traditional Release Coordination Basic Flow*

Key Risks and Mitigation

Risk	Impact	Mitigation
Version conflicts	Staging failures	Mandatory RC checklist + dependency map
Security gaps	Regulatory audit issues	Security scan + code review
Rollback uncertainty	Prolonged outage	Staging rollback rehearsal

Outcome

- The release was deployed without customer-impacting incidents.

- Audit evidence was complete and accepted during quarterly compliance review.

- Regression escape rate fell by 40%.

CHAPTER 2

Continuous Delivery Process

Overview

The Continuous Delivery Process is a structured set of inter- and intra-departmental steps and artifacts required for successful continuous integration, verification, authorization, and deployment of software services.

Continuous Delivery Model

The Hybrid Continuous Delivery Model includes three major processes:

- **Feature Release** – Coordinates customer-facing activities and documentation such as external notifications, marketing activities, feature activation flags controlling limited versus general availability, customer training, and new customer provisioning. The Feature Release Process initiates one or multiple Service Delivery processes.

Y. Kuznetsoff, *Building Robust IT Release Processes*, Apress Pocket Guides,
https://doi.org/10.1007/979-8-8688-2652-8_2

- **Service Delivery** – Coordinates continuous software development, verification, and integration using automated pipelines such as OpenShift Container Platform (OCP) or custom pipelines using Jenkins or other CI/CD solutions (e.g., GitLab CI, GitHub Actions, Azure DevOps). Its main purpose is to produce fully verified and authorized release candidate (RC) builds ready for deployment to multiple pre-production and production environments across multiple data centers and regions, if applicable. Service Delivery initiates one or multiple deployments.

- **Deployment** – Coordinates deployment procedures that distribute fully verified and authorized RC builds to target environments, including production. New functionality might be available to customers immediately after production deployment or can be enabled later as part of the customer-facing Feature Release Process.

Figure 2-1 illustrates the interactions among the Feature Release, Service Delivery, and Deployment processes. It also highlights the functions that initiate and coordinate major activities, while these activities may be executed by other functions.

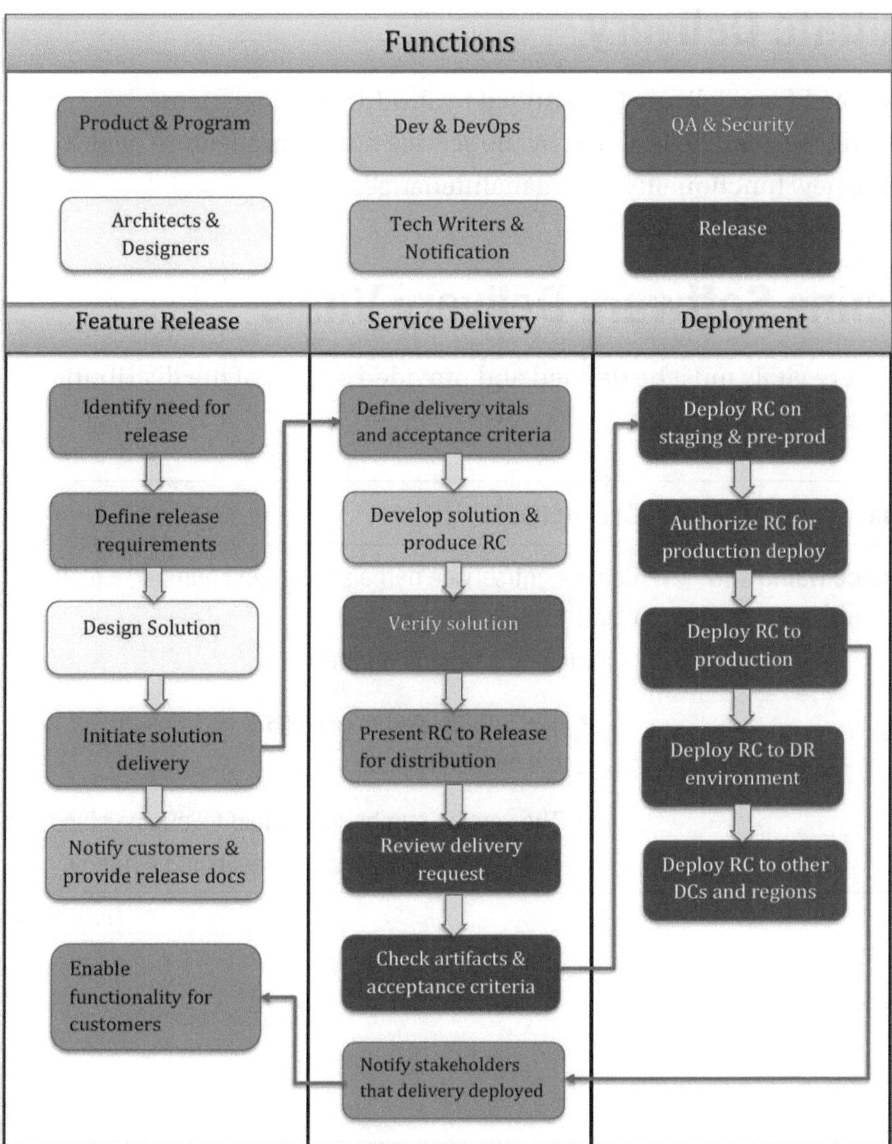

Figure 2-1. *Continuous Delivery Model*

Initiate Delivery

The need for a delivery is identified by Product Management.

Delivery can be initiated by the service owner as a feature or as a part of the new functionality or as a maintenance.

Define Software Delivery Vitals

Delivery vitals must be defined and provided as part of the distribution request.

Item	Description
Service Name and Version	Component/service name and version number, e.g., Hello World 1.0.0. In assigning a version number • The product owner assigns a version number for the service release. • The version numbering should follow the standards defined by engineering in versioning strategy.

(continued)

Item	Description
Delivery Type	Component/service delivery type is a mandatory value and should be determined by the development team following this guidance:

- **Major** – Significant functionality change for an existing service or introduction of a new service.

- **Minor** – Minor changes to functionality are added to an existing service.

- **Maintenance** – Does not add new functionality, typically used to solve not urgent issues and/or to perform regular maintenance.

- **Patch** – Resolves a specific issue that is necessary to address before the next scheduled delivery.

- **Hotfix** – Implements critical fixes or software changes that repair or prevent a service-impacting situation. Used only when an urgent issue needs to be addressed rapidly.

(continued)

Item	Description
Delivery Category	Delivery category refers to a class of delivery, which requires particular Delivery Acceptance Criteria. For example, delivery category can be Standard Delivery or Internal Delivery: a) Standard Delivery category applies when a development team delivers a new/updated service to production that will be used/accessed by customers or by other production services. Standard Delivery category applies to both general and limited availability of new functionality. Standard Delivery potentially can be a customer-facing release and should meet acceptance criteria related to company legal and contractual obligations as well as internal policies, e.g. notifications, customer training, what's new guide, etc. b) Internal Delivery category applies when a development team delivers a new or updated existing service in production that is not used by customers and does not have active downstream production dependencies. For example, the development team wants to pre-deploy and test new functionality on production infrastructure that won't be available to customers yet. Internal Delivery category should meet acceptance criteria related only to internal policies, e.g., security authorization, risk assessment, and QA approval

(continued)

Item	Description
Description	The delivery description should explain to the stakeholders what features/functionality (or part of) are being distributed to production. This should be written in such a way that the reader understands, in plain text, what the general intent of the delivery is. Avoid technical jargon where possible. Please note the description is utilized by other stakeholders, like tech writers, customer support, etc. Please include information pertaining to bug fixes if applicable.
Delivery Dependency	If delivery depends on any other delivery(s) or vice versa, all dependencies should be provided along with their versions. Only tested dependencies' version combination can be distributed to production. If this delivery depends on any infrastructure change that must be implemented either prior to or during or after the production deployment, corresponding infrastructure change ticket(s) should be attached to the Delivery Dependency field.
Potential Service Interruptions and Customer Impact	Information about planned service outage or any potential for even a brief service interruption must be provided. This info is mandatory. An impact analysis must be done for every delivery and stated in corresponding Internal and External Release Announcements.
RC Date	Date when the release candidate (RC) build is planned to be produced and fully verified.
Staging Deployment Date and Time	Date and time when the RC build is scheduled to be deployed on the staging environment.

(continued)

Item	Description
Production Deployment Date and Time	Date and time when the RC build is scheduled to be deployed on the production environment.
Deployment Duration	Estimated deployment event duration from deployment start to verification completion.
Delivery Contacts	Personnel who participate in authorization, deployment, and verification of new delivery, e.g., product owner, dev lead, DevOps, QA, etc.
Delivery Scope	Explicit list of changes distributed by the specified delivery, i.e., list of corresponding tickets that have been resolved as part of this delivery. This may be a link to the initial version of Internal Release Notes that should be provided for each RC.

Define Software Delivery Acceptance Criteria

To ensure data security, system integrity, and business continuity, also to make sure that all deliveries are distributed in accordance with company legal and contractual obligations, the following acceptance criteria should be met:

Item	Requirement	Artifacts
External Notification	Affected customers should be notified of every Standard Delivery that has material impact, i.e., service interruption, new or changed or fixed functionality, etc. A Customer Release Announcement should include production deployment date and time, delivery type, change description, and customer impact.	External notification ticket
Internal Notification	Affected internal teams and stakeholders should be notified about upcoming delivery. An Internal Release Announcement should include production deployment date and time, delivery type, change description, service interruption detail, and link to finalized Internal Release Notes.	Internal notification ticket
Staging Deployment	Each change *should* be implemented and tested on the staging environment before it hits production. The main goal of this exercise is to reproduce as closely as possible the production deployment, rollback, and post-deploy/rollback verification. As a result of the staging exercise, the RC build must be successfully deployed and verified in the staging environment. See section "Staging Deployment" for staging deployment procedure details. Release Management provides authorization and coordinates the deployment event.	Deployment ticket for staging deployment

(continued)

57

Item	Requirement	Artifacts
Security Approval	For each delivery, Security function must run security assessment and verification against the RC build. Once required security verification is passed, Security provides an approval for production distribution.	Release security approval ticket
QA Test Approval	For each delivery, QA function must complete all required testing. QA test artifacts must be closed before production deployment.	QA test ticket
Release Notes	For each delivery, Internal Release Notes must be created and reviewed by Support/Escalation function.	Internal Release Notes
Risk Acceptance	For each delivery, the product owner or their delegate should provide risk assessment and approval before production deployment.	Production risk acceptance artifact

(continued)

Item	Requirement	Artifacts
Production Deployment	Assigned release manager/coordinator must ensure that all corresponding acceptance criteria are met and provide authorization for specific deployment. Assigned release manager/coordinator coordinates the deployment event via the deployment communication channel. Assigned DevOps and QA must deploy and verify the authorized RC build on the production environment following deployment instructions. See section "Production Deployment" for production deployment procedure details. Once the deployment procedure has been done, the assigned release manager/coordinator should confirm either successful deployment completion or rollback and close the corresponding deployment ticket.	Deployment ticket for production deployment

Create a Software Delivery Request Task

To plan activities, track progress, manage deployments, and meet business, audit, and engineering requirements with full compliance, the development team lead must create a Software Delivery Request ticket based on the information defined above.

Create a Release Management Delivery Task

To efficiently assist the development team, Release Management must ensure that a Release Management Delivery ticket is created for each delivery. The ticket tracks the progress and completion of pre-delivery, delivery, and post-delivery items and tasks.

Execute Software Delivery Tasks

Execute a Software Delivery Request Task

Once the Software Delivery Request is created, the development team must execute all the delivery tasks listed in the delivery request and corresponding tickets/artifacts.

I recommend creating a master ticket for each delivery request where all corresponding tickets are attached. Also, the creation of all corresponding artifacts can be automated and common information transferred to dependent tickets automatically.

Execute a Release Management Software Delivery Task

The assigned release manager/coordinator ensures that all required items and tasks are executed to completion and that corresponding tickets are closed.

Deployment Process

Deployment is the act of making a software system available for use on a target environment. Deploying software is a function of engineering; however, multiple actions performed by multiple actors should be coordinated by the release manager/coordinator.

Deployment Potential Use Case Scenarios

- **Update an Existing Service** – Single production deployment to all affected data centers

- **Update an Existing Service** – Multiple production deployments, each for a specific region

- **Add a New Service That Meanwhile Will Not Be Used/ Accessed Either by Customers or by Other Services** – Single production internal deployment to all affected data centers

- **Update Multiple Existing Services** – Single production deployment to all affected data centers

- **Update Multiple Existing Services** – Multiple production deployments each for a specific region

- **Emergency Fix Existing Service** – Single production hotfix deployment to all affected data centers

If more than one component participates in the delivery, multi-component deployment orchestration and deployment sequence should be created and tested during the staging exercise.

Resync with the Production Environment

Once a new service version has been deployed to production, the same RC version must be re-deployed to staging (if not already deployed) to keep staging in sync with production and representative of its state.

Deployment Procedure

Deployment is a vital function of the delivery process and tracked in deployment ticket(s).

Staging Deployment

Each change *must* be implemented and tested on the staging environment before it hits production. The main goal of this exercise is to reproduce as close as possible production deployment, rollback, and post-deploy/rollback verification.

The staging exercise for all delivery types should include the following steps:

1) QA runs a pre-deploy automated smoke test to ensure that legacy issues will not be mixed with potential deployment issues (optional).

2) DevOps deploys new code and/or configuration change to the staging environment following deployment instructions.

3) QA runs a production-like post-deployment smoke test.

4) DevOps rolls back deployed code and/or configuration change to the previous version using rollback instructions (optional).

    a. QA runs a production-like post-rollback smoke test.

    b. DevOps re-deploys new code and/or configuration change to the staging environment again using finalized deployment instructions.

    c. QA runs a production-like post-deployment smoke test.

5) Release manager must close the corresponding deployment ticket after deployment has been completed.

Production Deployment

Production deployment procedure for all delivery types should include the following steps:

1) QA runs a pre-deploy automated smoke test to ensure that legacy issues will not be mixed with potential deployment issues (optional).

2) DevOps deploys new code and/or configuration change to the prod environment using deployment instructions.

3) QA runs a production post-deployment smoke test.

4) If post-deployment verification failed and cannot be troubleshooted, then

    a. DevOps rolls back deployed code and/or configuration change to the previous version using rollback instructions.

    b. QA runs a production post-rollback smoke test.

5) If post-deployment/rollback verification passed, the release manager/coordinator must state in the corresponding deployment ticket that new functionality either has been successfully deployed or rolled back and verified in production.

6) Release manager/coordinator must close the corresponding deployment ticket.

The rollback instructions must handle both scenarios:

1) A component cannot be completed and must be rolled back.

2) The component was successfully installed but a subsequent deployment failed, requiring the entire package to be rolled back.

Post-production Extended Verification

It is recommended to run post-production extended verification after deploying customer-facing services to production. This verification should be done by selected specialists from customer-facing functions (Support, Product, Marketing, etc.) who understand how customers will use the new functionality. This helps identify and fix deficiencies before customers encounter them.

Case Study: Continuous Delivery Transformation in a Global SaaS Company

Background

A global SaaS messaging platform handled billions of messages per day. Engineering teams committed to accelerating delivery to meet competitive demands but lacked standardized pipelines and reproducible environment provisioning.

Challenges

Multiple teams maintained inconsistent CI/CD workflows, infrastructure drift existed across staging and production, and deployments required manual approvals that slowed throughput.

Transformation Approach

The engineering organization aligned around a Continuous Delivery Model. Infrastructure was re-implemented using Infrastructure-as-Code (IaC); pipelines were consolidated into a single delivery framework with automated smoke tests, security checks, and deployment orchestration using GitOps principles.

Continuous Delivery Pipeline Architecture

Figure 2-2 illustrates the end-to-end flow of changes as they progress from source control through automated build and test, release candidate validation, and finally multi-region deployment.

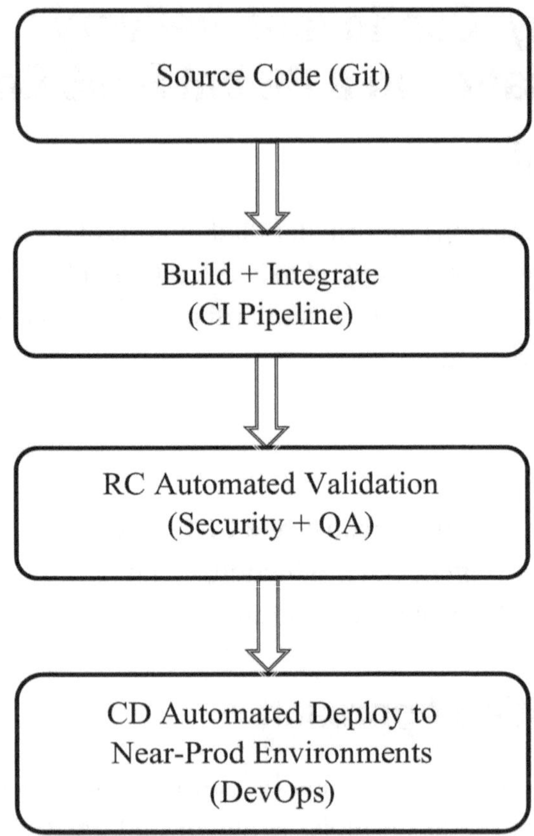

Figure 2-2. Continuous Delivery Pipeline

Outcome

Delivery velocity increased dramatically. Automated verification reduced human error and increased confidence in production deployments.

CHAPTER 3

Infrastructure Release Process

Overview

The infrastructure release process defines a structured and repeatable method for distributing infrastructure changes—such as operating system upgrades, database and middleware updates, network reconfiguration, capacity expansion, or deployment platform modifications—across all enterprise environments.

Unlike software releases, infrastructure releases focus on platform stability, scalability, performance, and operational continuity. However, the level of coordination, documentation, and governance should be **identical** to software releases. A consistent and well-defined approach reduces operational risk, supports compliance, and ensures that infrastructure remains reliable throughout Continuous Delivery cycles.

© Yuri Kuznetsoff 2026
Y. Kuznetsoff, *Building Robust IT Release Processes*, Apress Pocket Guides,
https://doi.org/10.1007/979-8-8688-2652-8_3

Infrastructure Release Process Objectives

The main objectives of the infrastructure release process are as follows:

- Ensure infrastructure stability and service continuity.

- Maintain platform reliability during changes by using controlled, versioned, and well-documented rollout procedures.

- Reduce operational risk through structured planning.

- Prevent unexpected outages by validating changes in pre-production environments and defining explicit rollback procedures.

- Align infrastructure updates with application and security requirements.

- Avoid mismatched versions, breaking changes, or configuration drift between application and infrastructure layers.

- Increase automation and repeatability.

- Ensure that complex changes—especially those implemented through Infrastructure-as-Code (IaC)—are consistent and reproducible.

- Improve auditability and compliance.

- Provide traceable documentation for all infrastructure changes to support internal and external audits.

Infrastructure Release Process Types

To efficiently deliver various infrastructure changes, define the following infrastructure release types.

Platform Upgrade

Distribution of updated operating systems, container runtimes, virtualization platforms, database engines, or middleware components.

Security and Compliance Update

Application of mandatory security patches, configuration hardening, vulnerability remediation, or certificate rotations.

Infrastructure Expansion or Migration

Addition of new data centers, network segments, storage volumes, or migration of workloads to new hardware or cloud regions.

Monitoring and Observability Update

Deployment or upgrade of monitoring agents, telemetry collectors, alerting systems, or logging pipelines.

Infrastructure-as-Code Delivery

Distribution of versioned configuration templates (Terraform, Ansible, Helm, CloudFormation) that modify shared infrastructure.

Define the Infrastructure Release Process

Determine the Infrastructure Release Model

Senior Operations Management should determine the release model based on infrastructure complexity, change frequency, automation maturity, and regulatory requirements. Common models include

a) **Scheduled Release Model**

   Infrastructure changes deployed on a predefined cadence (e.g., weekly maintenance window)
   Suitable for regulated industries and high-stability environments

b) **Continuous Infrastructure Delivery Model**

   Changes delivered frequently using automated IaC pipelines

   Suitable for mature DevOps organizations with strong automation and testing practices

Define Infrastructure Release Structure

Each infrastructure release should follow this general structure:

Stage	Description
Planning	Identify scope, dependencies, risks, and rollback options.
Pre-release validation	Deploy and test changes on representative pre-production environments.
Authorization	Obtain approvals from Security, Architecture, and Operations.
Execution	Implement changes in production with real-time coordination.
Post-deployment verification	Validate platform performance, security posture, and availability.
Documentation update	Update infrastructure records, diagrams, and configuration baselines.

Define Infrastructure Release Functions, Steps, and Artifacts

Figure 3-1 presents a decision tree used to classify infrastructure-related changes and determine the appropriate release function, workflow steps, and required artifacts.

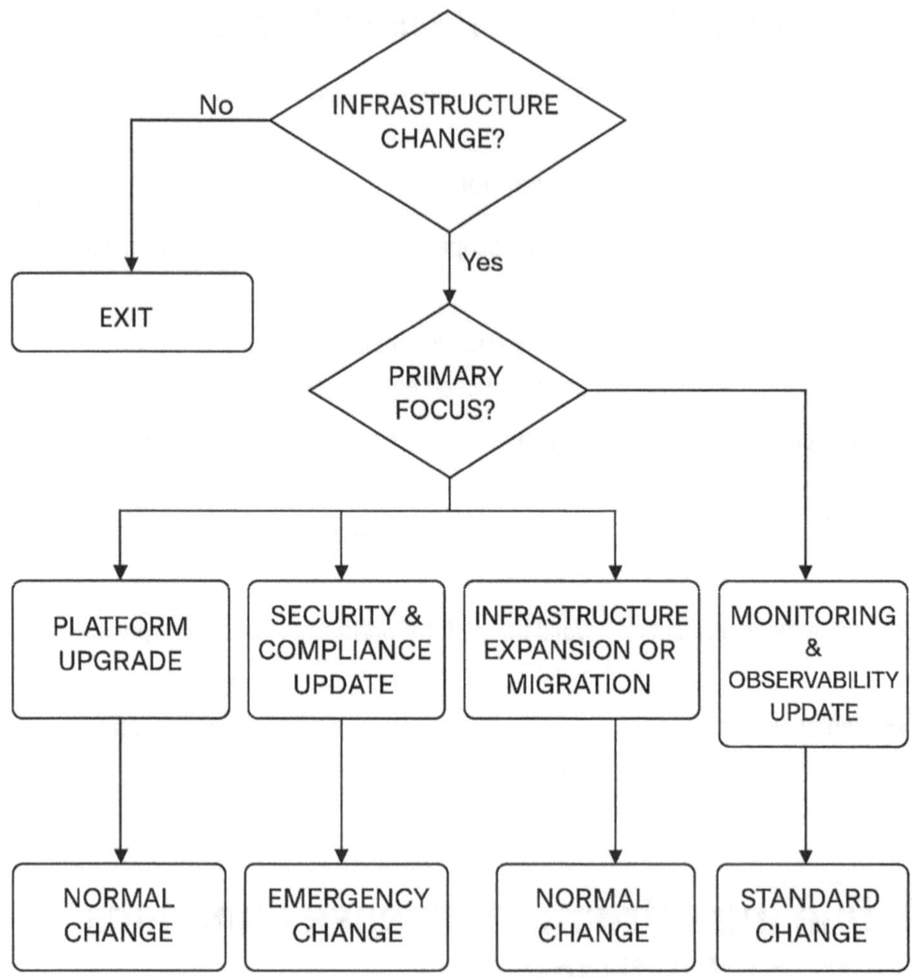

Figure 3-1. *Infrastructure Change Decision Tree*

Identify the Need for Infrastructure Change

An infrastructure change is triggered by

- Required OS, platform, database, or middleware upgrades

- Mandatory security patches or compliance deadlines

- Environment scalability requirements

- Hardware refresh cycles

- Audit findings or configuration drift

- Phase-in of new data centers or cloud regions

The infrastructure change request is typically initiated by Operations, Architecture, Engineering, or Security teams.

Define Infrastructure Change Requirements

Once the need for an infrastructure change is identified, infrastructure owners must define its characteristics.

Infrastructure change vitals should include

- Business driver

- Infrastructure component(s)

- Target environments

- Change description

- Dependencies

- Target dates

- Security and compliance requirements

- Estimated service impact

- Test requirements (functional, performance, security)

Determine Infrastructure Release Type

Use the categories defined in Chapter 1, section **Determine Release Type**. Select based on impact, complexity, and risk.

Determine Infrastructure Change Version

An infrastructure change should follow consistent versioning so it can be tracked, audited, and rolled back.

Recommended Practices

- Version labels must be fully qualified and reflect change category.

- Infrastructure version should be maintained in Configuration Management Database (CMDB) and Infrastructure-as-Code (IaC) repositories.

- Each version must map to exact configuration artifacts and IaC templates.

- Rollback version must be explicitly documented and tested.

Infrastructure Change Request

Each infrastructure change request must include

1. Change name and version

2. Change type

3. Change description

4. Scope of work

5. Dependencies (software, infrastructure, external vendors)

6. Target environments

7. Target date

8. Estimated deployment duration

9.   Service impact analysis

10.   Implementation contacts

11.   Security assessment requirements

Release Management, IT Operations, and Change Management review this information, validate feasibility, and determine scheduling options.

Infrastructure Release Plan

An Infrastructure Release Plan should be created by a release engineer and must include

1.   Summary of the infrastructure change

2.   All release milestones

3.   Environment-specific deployment instructions

4.   Pre-deployment validation steps

5.   Rollback plan

6.   Verification plan

7.   List of approvals required

8.   Risk assessment and mitigation strategies

Deployment procedure sequencing must be clearly documented for multi-data-center or cluster-wide updates.

Infrastructure Deployment

Pre-deployment Steps

1. Notify stakeholders about planned service interruptions, if applicable.

2. Validate availability of environment access, backups, snapshots, and failover capacity.

3. Confirm stability of dependent systems.

4. Create an infrastructure deployment communication channel.

5. Verify staging or sandbox testing is completed.

Deployment Steps

Infrastructure deployment must follow clear, explicit instructions. Typical steps include as follows:

1. Execute a pre-deployment smoke test.

2. Implement the infrastructure change following deployment (implementation) instructions.

3. Validate node health, cluster status, or service connectivity.

4. Monitor CPU, memory, disk, and network performance in real time.

5. Record all actions in the deployment communication channel.

Rollback Steps

Rollback instructions must be defined, tested, and included in the deployment ticket.

Rollback Scenarios

- Deployment fails prior to completion.

- Deployment completes, but post-deployment verification fails.

- Stakeholders identify delayed-impact issues requiring full rollback.

Rollback steps must restore previous versions of

- Configurations

- IaC templates

- System snapshots

- Cluster or node state

- QA or ops must complete post-rollback verification.

Pre-production and Validation Environments

Infrastructure changes should be validated on the following environments, as applicable:

- Sandbox

- Integration QA

- Performance test

- Staging

The staging environment must be as close to production as possible and must support

- Full deployment

- Rollback

- Failure simulation

- Configuration verification

Infrastructure Verification and Authorization

Functional Verification

IT Operations and/or QA verifies baseline functionality after infrastructure modification. Stable production software should be used to test infrastructure change.

Performance Validation

Validate resource consumption, latency, throughput, and scaling behavior.

Security Validation

Security must

- Review change scope.

- Validate configuration hardening.

- Run vulnerability scans.

- Provide security approval for production deployment.

Open Issue Review

All known defects and risks must be reviewed and approved prior to the Go/NoGo decision.

Risk Management

Each infrastructure change must include

- Risk identification

- Impact assessment

- Mitigation strategy

- Rollback readiness review

Product and infrastructure owners must review all open risks prior to deployment.

Production Deployment

Production deployment must follow the explicit Infrastructure Deployment Plan.

Key Activities

- Pre-deploy a smoke test.

- Execute deployment.

- Validate environment health.

- Execute rollback (if required).

- Confirm results with stakeholders.

- Update all artifacts and CMDB entries.

All deployment events must be recorded for audit and retrospective purposes.

Release Retrospective

After high-impact or complex infrastructure releases, conduct a Retrospective Meeting to evaluate

- What worked well

- What issues occurred

- Root cause analysis

- Recommendations for process improvements

Lessons learned must be applied to future releases. They are reviewed during the Retrospective Meeting and translated into concrete actions. Depending on the nature of the finding, updates may be applied to test plans, risk assessments, deployment instructions, validation steps, or other release artifacts. When a systemic gap is identified, the infrastructure release process and its plans are updated accordingly to prevent recurrence.

Maintain an Infrastructure Change Tracker

An Infrastructure Release Tracker should include

- Change Name

- Release Version

- Release Type

- Target Date

- Deployment Date

- Status

- Link to Release and Deployment Plan

- Rollback Result (if applicable)

Statuses should match software release statuses (PENDING, WIP, COMPLETE, PARKED, MERGED, ROLLEDBACK).

Case Study: Infrastructure Change Failure and Recovery

Background

A multinational enterprise attempted a global OS upgrade across clusters hosting mission-critical workloads. While most regions succeeded, one region experienced node instability.

Root Cause Analysis

A kernel parameter inconsistency created incompatibility with the workload scheduler. Although staging was updated, rollback procedures were incomplete, delaying recovery.

- **Symptom**

  The issue first appeared as intermittent node instability in one region, with workloads failing to schedule reliably. At this stage, the failures looked transient and not tied to any specific hardware component.

- **Investigation**

  Initial diagnostics focused on hardware health and cluster connectivity, but no faults were detected. The team then compared OS-level behavior between stable and unstable nodes. System logs showed scheduler-related errors that did not appear in other regions. A parameter-by-parameter comparison of kernel settings revealed a mismatch introduced during the upgrade.

- **Findings**

  The affected nodes were running a kernel parameter configuration that differed from both the staging environment and the successfully upgraded regions. This discrepancy caused an incompatibility with the workload scheduler, triggering instability under production load.

- **Root Cause**

  A kernel parameter inconsistency introduced during the OS upgrade created a scheduler incompatibility, leading to node instability.

- **Contributing Factor**

  Rollback procedures were incomplete, which extended the time required to restore the region to a stable state.

Infrastructure Upgrade Failure Sequence

Figure 3-2 illustrates a typical failure progression during an infrastructure upgrade.

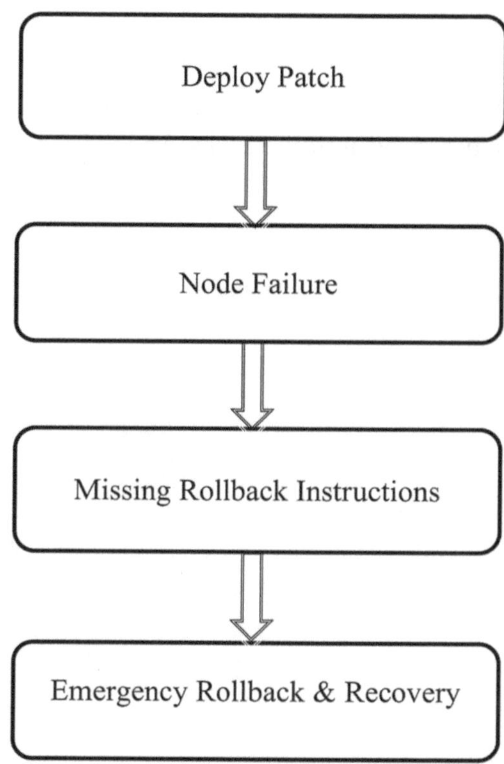

Figure 3-2. Infrastructure Upgrade Failure Sequence

Infrastructure Governance Gaps

Gap	Impact	Correction
No rollback validation	Delayed recovery	Mandatory rollback testing
Drift in kernel params	Node instability	IaC-enforced baselines
No pre-prod performance testing	Capacity issues	Performance validation stage

Outcome

Rollback succeeded and guided major improvements: explicit rollback templates, pre-production checks, and more rigorous change governance.

CHAPTER 4

Disaster Recovery Procedure

Overview

- Disaster Recovery (DR) is a critical extension of release and deployment processes. Its goal is to restore service availability following catastrophic infrastructure or application failures that cause prolonged outages or significant degradation of service.

- A Disaster Recovery Procedure ensures that:

  - Critical systems are fully recoverable.

  - Recovery meets business-defined timelines (RTO/RPO).

  - Failover operations are safe, repeatable, and auditable.

  - Teams know their roles, communication channels, and escalation rules.

- DR must integrate with both the **infrastructure release process** and **software release process** to ensure full operational continuity.

© Yuri Kuznetsoff 2026

Y. Kuznetsoff, *Building Robust IT Release Processes*, Apress Pocket Guides,
https://doi.org/10.1007/979-8-8688-2652-8_4

Objectives

The main objectives of Disaster Recovery are as follows:

- Restore critical applications and infrastructure to operational state.

- Minimize service disruption and business impact.

- Protect and recover data without corruption or loss beyond approved thresholds.

- Ensure high availability through automated failover systems where applicable.

- Comply with legal, regulatory, and customer service-level agreements.

Key Terminology

- **RTO (Recovery Time Objective)** – Maximum acceptable time to restore service

- **RPO (Recovery Point Objective)** – Maximum acceptable data loss measured in time

- **Primary Site** – Active production location

- **Secondary DR Site** – Backup environment prepared for failover

- **Failover** – Switching active traffic to DR site

- **Failback** – Returning operations to Primary Site when stable

DR Governance and Authorization

Disaster Recovery must follow a defined governance structure:

Role	Responsibility
Business continuity (BC) manager	Accountable for DR policy and alignment with the Business Continuity Plan (BCP)
Product owner	Approves service-specific DR requirements
IT Operations	Executes infrastructure failover and restoration
DevOps	Restores application, configuration, and deployment pipelines
Security lead	Validates restored state meets compliance standards
Support lead	Coordinates communication to internal/external users

All DR events require a **Go/No-Go** decision from the BC manager and product owner.

DR Types

The DR execution model varies based on severity and recovery needs:

- **Planned DR Exercise** – Testing system failover capabilities

- **Emergency Failover** – Unexpected outage with immediate activation

- **Partial Recovery** – Scoped recovery of degraded services

DR Procedure

Disaster Recovery must follow a structured, documented process.

DR Trigger and Assessment

Triggers may include:

- Full data center failure or network isolation

- Critical infrastructure outage

- Ransomware or other security events rendering systems inoperable

- Widespread data corruption or integrity issues

Steps

1. Incident commander declares DR trigger.

2. Business impact analysis determines DR Tier (Critical/High/Medium).

3. BC manager activates DR Procedure.

4. Failover decision is recorded in DR event ticket.

Failover Execution

1. Confirm last validated backup or replication state.

2. Initiate failover procedure according to runbook.

3. Validate

   a. Application start-up success

   b. Network connectivity

   c. Authentication and authorization systems

4. Update routing/DNS/load balancers.

5. Monitor platform for the defined stabilization period.

DR Communication Plan

Communication is coordinated by the support lead.

Audience	Timeline	Method
Internal teams	Immediately after activation	Incident channel/email
Customers	As defined in SLA	Status page notification
Executives	Immediately	Phone/email escalation

Failback Procedure

Failback occurs when

- Primary Site stability is verified.

- Root cause is resolved.

- Risk assessment is completed.

Failback Steps

1. Restore replication direction.

2. Validate data, configuration, and performance.

3. Switch traffic back to primary.

4. Close the DR event ticket after retrospective.

DR Runbook Requirements

Each production service must maintain a **Service DR Runbook** including

- Service description and architecture diagram
- Dependencies and required infrastructure components
- Data replication configuration and validation process
- Step-by-step failover and failback actions
- Verification scenarios
- Known failure modes
- DR tests and results record

DR Testing and Validation

To Ensure Readiness

- **Annual DR tests** required for critical services
- **Quarterly validation** of backup integrity
- **Automated failover drills** for cloud platforms where applicable

All tests must be

- Documented
- Reviewed by the BC manager
- Signed off by product owner(s)

DR Risk Management

Key Risk Categories

- **Replication Lag/Backup Failure** – Mitigate with monitoring + automated alerts.

- **Configuration Drift Between Environments** – Validate using IaC consistency checks.

- **Application Incompatibility During Failover** – Continuous DR readiness testing.

Unmitigated risks must be formally **accepted** before production launch.

DR Process Flow Diagram

Figure 4-1 ensures DR integrates with both software and infrastructure release processes by leveraging validated release artifacts and deployment automation.

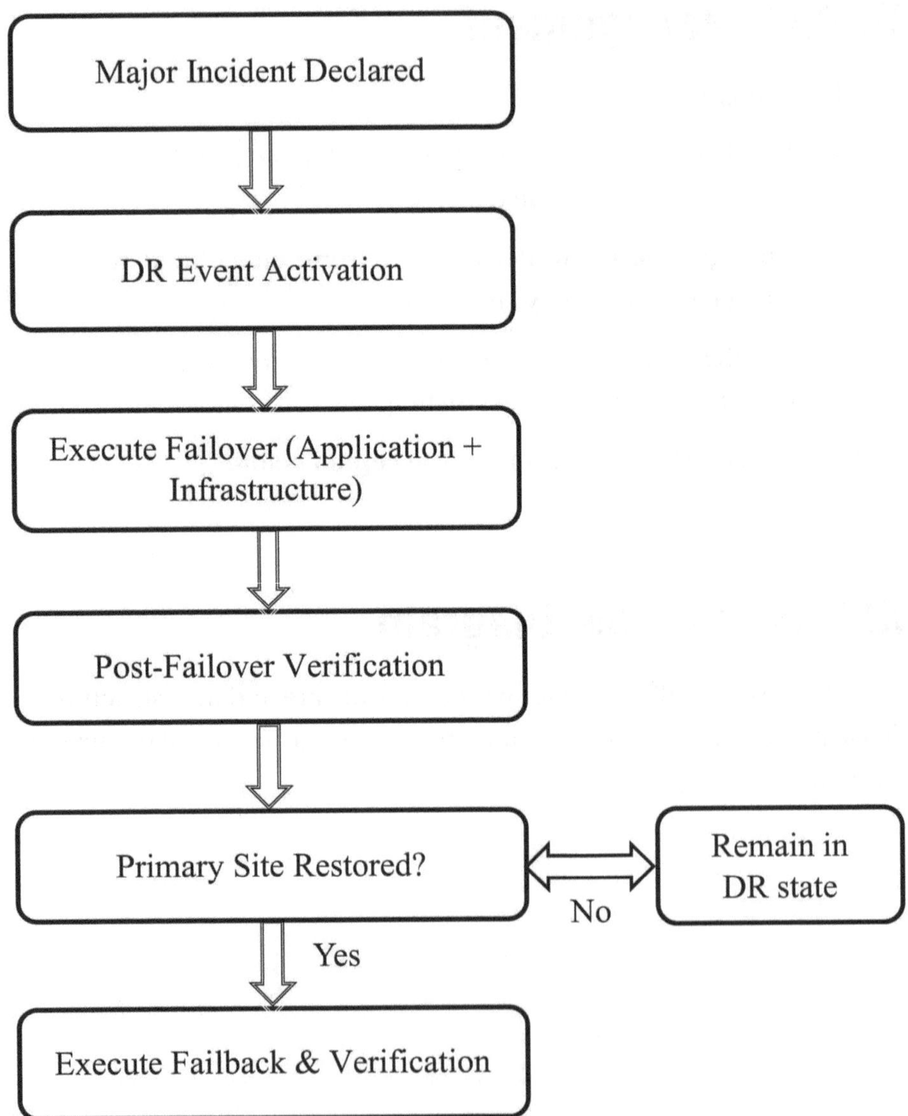

Figure 4-1. *Disaster Recovery Process Flow*

Failover Decision Matrix

Scenario	DR Trigger	Failover Required?	Primary Decision Owner	Notes
Full data center outage	Production unreachable	Yes—immediate	Incident commander	Auto-failover if supported.
Security breach resulting in system lockdown	Data compromised	Yes—emergency	Security lead + BC manager	Forensic containment required.
Partial application failure (critical service)	Customer impact	Conditional	Product owner	Consider rapid patch instead of DR activation.
Infrastructure upgrade failure	Post-change instability	Conditional	Release manager	Rollback may resolve issue.
Network isolation between sites	Regional outage	Yes	Network Operations	Prioritize traffic rerouting.

Service Tiering Model

Tier	Description	Example Services	Target RTO	Target RPO
Tier 1—Critical	Direct customer or regulatory impact, high financial loss	Authentication, transaction processing	$\leq$15 min	$\leq$5 min
Tier 2—High	High internal impact, reduced operational capability	Messaging, reporting	$\leq$1 hour	$\leq$30 min

(continued)

Tier	Description	Example Services	Target RTO	Target RPO
Tier 3— Medium	Non-customer-facing delays acceptable	Back-office tools	$\leq$4 hours	$\leq$2 hours
Tier 4— Low	No immediate operational impact	Internal analytics	$\leq$24 hours	$\geq$24 hours

Tier assignment must be approved by the business continuity manager and referenced in BC Documentation.

Regulatory Alignment

This DR framework aligns with

- **NIST SP 800-34 Rev.1** – Contingency Planning Guide for Federal Information Systems

- **ISO/IEC 22301** – Business Continuity Management Systems

- **SOC 2 Trust Services Criteria** – Availability and Security

- **ITIL Service Continuity Management**

Compliance checkpoints are integrated into **DR Authorization** steps to ensure

- Documented recovery controls

- Periodic DR testing audits

- Data protection and integrity validation

Disaster Recovery Maturity Assessment

A maturity model helps organizations evaluate readiness over time.

Level	Title	Characteristics	Action Focus
1—Initial	Ad Hoc Response	Minimal documentation, reactive recovery	Define DR policies and runbooks.
2—Developing	Structured Recovery	Inconsistent testing, manual failover	Improve automation and tracking.
3—Defined	Standardized DR	Runbooks validated annually	Integrate with release processes.
4—Managed	Measured and Governed	RTO/RPO tracked, compliance reporting	Optimize testing, performance, security.
5—Optimized	Full Resilience	Auto-failover, continuous validation	Predictive recovery, chaos, and resilience engineering.

Organizations should target **Level 3+** for mission-critical systems.

DR Plan Template

Section	Content
Service Name	Full component name and owner
DR Tier	Critical/High/Medium/Low
RTO/RPO	Measured target values
Dependencies	Services, databases, platforms, integrations
Backup Standard	Snapshot/replication details + frequency

(continued)

Section	Content
Failover Steps	Explicit runbook reference
Verification Steps	Functional/performance/security tests
Failback Steps	Primary restoration and validation
Contacts	Engineering, Ops, Security, Support
Audit References	NIST, ISO 22301, SOC 2 controls

DR Retrospective

- Performed after **every** DR event or exercise

- Review must include

    - Root cause and contributing factors

    - Timeline of recovery execution

    - RTO/RPO results versus targets

    - Effectiveness of communications

    - Action items for remediation

Case Study: Disaster Recovery Activation After a Regional Cloud Outage

Background

A mission-critical SaaS system experienced a cloud provider regional outage affecting authentication, messaging, and routing layers. Traffic had to be shifted to the DR region.

Challenges

Replication lag exceeded the RPO during initial assessment, and DR runbooks had not been updated for several months.

Failover Flow During DR Event

Figure 4-2 outlines the sequence of actions taken during a Disaster Recovery failover.

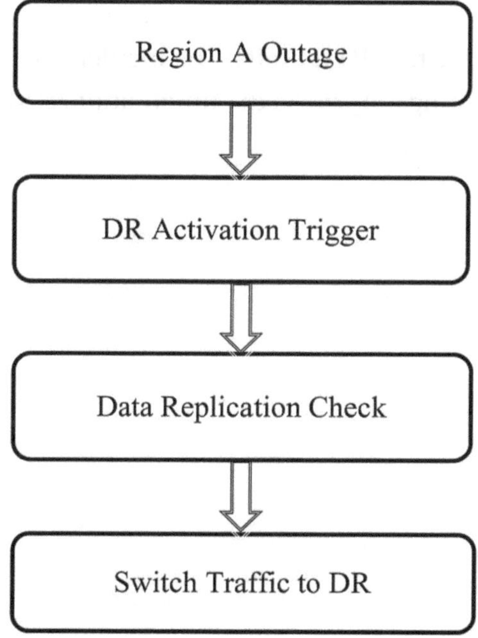

Figure 4-2. *Failover Flow During DR Event*

DR Metrics

Metric	Target	Actual
RTO	60 min	40 min
RPO	5 min	9 min
Failover duration	N/A	12 min

Outcome

Service was restored within RTO limits. The incident accelerated adoption of continuous DR testing, improved documentation, and bidirectional replication enhancements.

CHAPTER 5

Conclusion

In today's fast-paced and increasingly complex digital ecosystem, the ability to deliver software and infrastructure changes reliably and securely is not simply an operational goal—it is a strategic necessity. Throughout this book, we explored the full lifecycle of a robust IT release process, offering a practical, field-tested blueprint for transforming how organizations plan, execute, validate, and govern releases across diverse environments.

At the heart of this work lies a simple principle: **every release is an opportunity to build trust**. Trust—from customers, stakeholders, and internal teams—is earned through consistent execution, transparent communication, and disciplined governance. A well-structured release process provides the foundation for that trust.

From Framework to Culture

A release process is more than a set of steps or documents—it reflects a mindset and a culture. It reinforces the belief that quality is non-negotiable, that roles and responsibilities matter, and that every deployment represents a moment where engineering, operations, and business objectives converge. Whether delivering a new feature, deploying a configuration change, upgrading infrastructure, or executing a DR failover, the principles in this guide provide a path to doing so with clarity and confidence.

Applying What You've Learned

To begin adopting or strengthening your release processes, consider the following actionable steps:

- **Start Small** – Pilot the framework with one team, service, or product line to validate assumptions and refine workflows.

- **Customize Intentionally** – Adapt artifacts, gates, and acceptance criteria to align with your organization's risk profile, technology stack, and operational maturity.

- **Educate Continuously** – Share the release framework across development, QA, DevOps, security, and support functions to establish a common language and shared expectations.

- **Iterate with Purpose** – Use retrospectives, KPIs, and incident learnings to continuously evolve and improve release processes.

Final Thought

A successful release is never just about code. It is about coordination, clarity, and both collective and personal responsibility. By investing in your release process, you are investing in predictability, resilience, and trust. The tools, models, templates, and governance practices in this guide are designed to help you build that trust—one release at a time.

General Recommendations

Avoid Mixed Variables

There are two situations where you can have mixed variables during deployment:

A) Both infrastructure and software changes were deployed simultaneously.

In this case if you encounter an issue during the deployment or verification, it is hard to identify the root cause of the issue and would take much time and efforts to troubleshoot it.

Normally you test new software against stable and verified infrastructure. Also, you test new infrastructure against stable and verified software. If you have both software and infrastructure unstable and not separately verified, your test is not fully representative.

B) An old issue affects new functionality verification.

In this case when QA verifies new functionality right after the deployment, they may hit an issue that inherited from the previous application version. In most cases it is not so obvious that it is a legacy issue and takes a lot of time and effort to identify that.

Y. Kuznetsoff, *Building Robust IT Release Processes*, Apress Pocket Guides,
https://doi.org/10.1007/979-8-8688-2652-8

The best way to prevent extensive troubleshooting is to run a pre-deployment smoke test to identify existing issues and distinguish them from new issues during post-deployment verification.

Streamline a Sophisticated Process

To streamline a sophisticated process, you cannot just simplify it; however, you can organize it in a way that the process can be well managed and automated. Automation is as good as the process it automates. Any attempts to automate a poorly defined process result in time-consuming troubleshooting.

Define an Outage Window

If anticipating business or service impact during production deployment, run the deployment within an agreed outage window to minimize impact.

Maintain Feature Flags

Feature flags (or feature toggles) are mechanisms that let teams control the availability of specific functionality at runtime without deploying new code. They are commonly used to support limited or general availability releases, experimentation, and gradual rollouts.

a) Avoid leaving stale flags in the codebase—they become technical debt.

b) Use standardized, descriptive names to clarify purpose and ownership.

c) Assign each flag to a responsible team or engineers.

Create Role-Based Responsibility Matrix (RACI)

This matrix clarifies who is Responsible, Accountable, Consulted, and Informed across key release activities:

Activity	Product Owner	Release Manager	QA Lead	DevOps	Security Lead	Stakeholders
Define release scope	A	C	I	I	I	I
Create Release Vitals	R	C	I	I	I	I
Build release candidate	I	C	C	R	I	I
QA verification	I	C	R	C	I	I
Security assessment	I	C	I	I	R	I
Risk assessment	R	C	C	I	C	I
Final approval (Go/NoGo)	A	R	C	C	C	C
Deployment execution	I	A	C	R	I	I
Internal Release Notes	R	C	R	I	I	I
Customer notification	R	C	I	I	I	I
Retrospective review	A	R	C	C	C	C

Assess Release Quality KPIs

These KPIs help monitor and improve the reliability, efficiency, and governance of your release process:

KPI	Description
% of Successful Deployments	Ratio of deployments completed without rollback or major incident
% of Releases Delivered on Time	Measures adherence to planned release schedules
% of Releases with Verified RCs	Tracks how many releases had fully verified release candidates before deploy
% of Releases with Rollbacks	Indicates stability issues or gaps in pre-deployment testing
% of Releases with QA Sign-Off	Ensures Quality Assurance validation is consistently applied
% of Releases with Security Approval	Tracks compliance with security verification protocols
Mean Time to Deploy (MTTD)	Average time taken to complete a deployment
Mean Time to Recover (MTTR)	Average time to restore service after a failed deployment
% of Releases with Risk Assessment	Ensures risk mitigation is part of the release planning
% of Releases with Complete Artifacts	Measures completeness of documentation (plans, notes, checklists, etc.)

Use a Staging Environment for Disaster Recovery (DR) Exercises

A staging environment should not be used solely for pre-production deployment validation. It also plays a critical role in validating the organization's Disaster Recovery (DR) readiness. Because staging is typically the closest representation of the production environment, it provides a safe, controlled, and cost-efficient platform to simulate DR scenarios without affecting customers or operational workloads.

Using staging for DR exercises helps prevent configuration drift between environments, ensures the DR site can support real workloads, and validates that teams are trained in real failover and failback execution.

Rehearse Failover and Failback Using Staging

Staging should be configured to mirror production's network topology, authentication, deployment pipelines, and data access patterns. This allows Operations, DevOps, and Security teams to practice

- Full application failover

- Infrastructure failover (compute, storage, network)

- DNS/routing updates

- Authentication and authorization validation

- Failback to primary once stability is restored

This rehearsal ensures that runbooks are complete, sequencing is correct, and automation behaves the same way it will in production.

Validate DR Runbooks End to End

DR runbooks should be executed on staging exactly as written.Exercises must confirm the following:

- Steps are correct and executable.

- No assumptions rely on undocumented knowledge.

- Automation scripts are functional and version-aligned.

- Verification tests detect both success and failure conditions.

Staging exercises often reveal missing dependencies, incorrect sequence ordering, or configuration inconsistencies that would cause an actual DR failover to stall.

Test Replication and Data Integrity on Staging

Whenever feasible, replicate realistic datasets to staging to validate

- Data replication or snapshot mechanisms

- RTO/RPO assumptions

- Backup restoration steps

- Schema and configuration compatibility

This ensures the DR site can support real operational loads and that no silent data corruption exists before a real failover.

Validate Infrastructure Changes Against DR Procedures

Any significant infrastructure or platform update (OS patching, DB upgrade, container runtime upgrade, middleware update) should be DR-tested on staging before production deployment.

If a new version cannot fail over and fail back cleanly in staging, it should **not** be deployed to production.

Confirm DR Site Compatibility

Staging must confirm that the DR region or DR cluster can

- Boot all services successfully.

- Apply required configuration and secrets.

- Maintain expected performance and latency.

- Pass functional, performance, and security verification.

This provides strong evidence for audit and compliance frameworks (e.g., ISO 22301, SOC 2).

Integrate DR Exercises into Release Cycles

I recommend coupling DR exercises with high-impact releases such as

- Major infrastructure upgrades

- Significant application architecture changes

- Platform migrations

- New DR region or cluster enablement

This reduces risk by validating that both the new version and the existing DR procedures work together.

Procedure Checkpoints: A Quick Reference

This is a handy summary of operational decisions, key artifacts, roles, and approval gates.

1) **Operational Decision Frameworks**

   This section defines explicit decision frameworks used to guide release, deployment, and recovery decisions under operational pressure.

   - **Hotfix versus Rollback versus Disaster Recovery Decision Framework**

     a) **Conditions**

Condition	Hotfix	Rollback	Disaster Recovery
Issue affects a single component	Preferred	If hotfix unavailable	Not appropriate
Issue introduced by current release only	Risky	Preferred	Not appropriate
Issue impacts multiple services	Unsafe	Temporary	Only if infrastructure-related
Data corruption detected	Never	Insufficient	Required

(continued)

© Yuri Kuznetsoff 2026

Y. Kuznetsoff, *Building Robust IT Release Processes*, Apress Pocket Guides,
https://doi.org/10.1007/979-8-8688-2652-8

Condition	Hotfix	Rollback	Disaster Recovery
Security breach or active exploit	Only as containment	If safe	Required
Platform/region outage	Ineffective	Ineffective	Required
Fix is well-tested and isolated	Yes	No need	No
Root cause unknown	Dangerous	Temporary	Consider
Regulatory/audit impact	Requires approval	Requires approval	Often mandatory

b)   **Action Definitions**

Action	Purpose	Risk Level	Key Requirement
Hotfix	Correct isolated defect without reverting release	Medium–High	Fully tested, isolated change
Rollback	Restore previous known-good state	Low–Medium	Validated rollback plan
Disaster Recovery	Restore service after catastrophic failure	High	DR runbook + BC authorization

- **Conditions Where Continuous Delivery Is Unsafe**

  Continuous Delivery is unsafe when failure impact exceeds the team's ability to detect, isolate, and recover automatically.

Condition	CD Allowed	Rationale
Regulated production environment	Conditional	Requires gated approvals
Database schema change	No	High integrity risk
No automated rollback	No	Recovery not guaranteed
Strong observability and alerting	Yes	Early failure detection
Shared monolithic architecture	No	Coupled failure domains
Infrastructure and app changes bundled	No	Debugging complexity
No staging parity with production	No	False confidence
Formal Release Authorization present	Yes	Audit and accountability

- **Mandatory Release Blocking Conditions**

Condition	Block Release	Reason
Failed staging deployment	Always	Production parity broken
Security approval missing	Always	Compliance violation
Rollback untested	Depends on urgency	No recovery path
QA verification incomplete	Always	Quality risk
Data migration irreversible	Always	No recovery path

- **Authority Escalation Matrix**

Decision	Product Owner	Release Manager	DevOps	Security	BC Manager
Go/NoGo	Approve	Owner	Support	Support	No
Emergency code hotfix	Owner	Approve	Execute	Support	No
Emergency security patch	Advisory	Approve	Execute	Owner	No
Rollback	Owner	Approve	Execute	Advisory	No
DR activation	No	Advisory	Execute	Support	Owner

2) **Key Artifacts**

- **Software Release Artifacts**

    - **Release Vitals** – Business drivers, scope, teams, timelines

    - **Release Plan** – Milestones, work items, owners, approvals

    - **Deployment Plan** – Pre/post steps, deployment/rollback instructions

    - **Internal Release Notes** – Features, fixes, known issues

    - **RC Acceptance Checklist** – Verification and readiness criteria

    - **Risk Assessment** – Identified risks and mitigation strategies

- **Infrastructure Release Artifacts**

  - **Infrastructure Release Plan** – Change scope, environment readiness, deployment/rollback strategy

  - **Infrastructure Deployment Instructions** – Platform-specific steps and validation procedures

  - **Infrastructure Verification Checklist** – Functional, performance, security, and configuration checks

  - **Infrastructure Change Tracker** – Record of change type, environment, owner, results

- **Disaster Recovery (DR) Artifacts**

  - **DR Plan Template** – Service tier, RTO/RPO targets, dependencies, failover/failback procedures

  - **DR Runbook** – Step-by-step operational instructions for executing DR events

  - **Failover Decision Matrix** – Criteria and conditions for DR activation

  - **DR Test and Validation Checklist** – Replication checks, data integrity, failover/failback rehearsal

  - **DR Retrospective Report** – Root cause, timeline, RTO/RPO results, corrective actions

3) **Key Roles**

- **Product Owner** – Defines scope, owns risk and customer communication

- **Release Manager** – Coordinates process, approvals, and execution

- **QA Lead** – Verifies functionality, performance, and regression

- **DevOps** – Executes deployment and rollback procedures

- **Security Lead** – Assesses and approves security posture

- **Stakeholders** – Review and sign-off at key gates

4) **Approval Gates**

- QA sign-off

- Security approval

- Risk acceptance

- Final Go/NoGo decision

- Stakeholder review (for major releases)